RAW FOOD
QUICK & EASY

OVER **100** HEALTHY RECIPES

RAW FOOD
QUICK & EASY

OVER **100** HEALTHY RECIPES

Mary Rydman

hatherleigh

Hatherleigh Press is committed to preserving and protecting the natural resources of the Earth. Environmentally responsible and sustainable practices are embraced within the company's mission statement.

Hatherleigh Press is a member of the Publishers Earth Alliance, committed to preserving and protecting the natural resources of the planet while developing a sustainable business model for the book publishing industry.

www.hatherleighpress.com

Library of Congress Cataloging-in-Publication Data
Rydman, Mary
Raw food quick & easy : over 100 healthy recipes / Mary Rydman Hatherleigh.
   p. cm.
ISBN 978-1-57826-306-6 (hardcover : alk. paper) 1. Raw food diet—Recipes. 2. Quick and easy cookery. I. Title.
RM237.5.R93 2009
641.5'55—dc22
            2009018454

Raw Food Quick & Easy is available for bulk purchase, special promotions, and premiums. For information on reselling and special purchase opportunities, call 1-800-528-2550 and ask for the Special Sales Manager.

Interior Design by DCDesigns

10 9 8 7 6 5 4 3 2 1

Printed in the United States

))) hatherleigh

CONTENTS

INTRODUCTION   1

A NOTE FROM THE AUTHOR: MY STORY   5

CHAPTER 1:   SOAKING, SPROUTING AND STORING   9

CHAPTER 2:   ABOUT DEHYDRATING   15

CHAPTER 3:   THE RAW KITCHEN   17

CHAPTER 4:   IS IT REALLY RAW?   19

CHAPTER 5:   SIMPLE WAYS TO BOOST YOUR
             NUTRITION INTAKE   23

CHAPTER 6:   EATING ACCORDING TO OUR
             BIOLOGICAL DESIGN   27

CHAPTER 7:   FOOD AND EMOTIONS   29

CHAPTER 8:   THE RECIPES   35

             The 5 Element Smoothie and Other
             Breakfast Foods   35

             Beverages   41

             Dressings   47

             Sauces and Gravies   55

Salads   65

Dehydrated Crackers   81

Soups   93

Raw Dairy   103

Pâtés   107

Sides and Hearty Creations   117

Snacks and Finger Foods   135

Desserts   141

Ice Cream   161

APPENDIX: SOURCES   169

             ABOUT THE AUTHOR   171

CONTENTS

INTRODUCTION

Today's Americans are fortunate to live longer than any generation before us. Advances in science, medicine, and quality of life have led to a dynamic increase in lifespan. With more years ahead of us we can look forward to leading productive, adventurous and exciting lives through our sixties, seventies, and even into our eighties and nineties.

Having this new frontier before us, it's clear that the health of our minds and bodies is paramount. However, many of us are coming to realize that we can't rely solely on conventional healthcare in order keep us in optimum mental and physical health. Rather, we are choosing new, broader approaches to healthcare that cultivate a total health, body/mind connection, such as yoga, qigong, and meditation. Furthermore, many of us are going one step further and thinking more deeply about what we put in our bodies. How can we get the most benefit from our fruits and vegetables? As we age, making good choices about what we eat becomes more and more important.

One way to guard your health and your future is to choose raw foods. "Eating raw" doesn't have to mean never eating meat again, or refusing to cook anything, ever. Instead, you can incorporate raw foods into your regular diet as a means to boost your intake of key vitamins, minerals, and antioxidants. Eating raw has numerous benefits and can result in miraculous improvements in your overall health. Once you start to eat more raw foods, you'll notice an increase in energy and vitality—simply put, you'll begin to feel ten, twenty or even thirty years younger!

The movement towards raw food is not only a trend in awareness of what creates health for the body (and the earth), but a realization that these foods can actually taste good! My goal with this book is to provide fairly simple, easy to reproduce recipes that taste great. I do not like to spend hours and hours in the kitchen—and the majority of these recipes have been written for those who feel the same way. These recipes are guaranteed to surprise anyone who never imagined they could create tasty, filling, un-cooked meals. Some of these meals do take some planning, but with prac-tice you will remember to soak your nuts and seeds ahead of time just as you would plan ahead for any other meal. Eating raw is just a different type of planning and before you know, it will become second nature.

THE IMPORTANCE OF SIMPLICITY

One of the things that I find important and appreciate in daily food prepa-ration is simplicity. Often my dinner is a large salad with one of the dress-ings in this book—truly a meal in itself. Given that there are other books with gourmet live food preparation ideas, I have tried to present some reci-pes that are relatively simple, but still very delicious and filling. The more live food you include in your diet, the more simple flavors are appreciated, so there is less need for a lot of time-consuming preparations.

There are times when you will need a chunk of time to prepare some-thing such as crackers. Taking a couple hours to prepare some dehydrated crackers is well worth it as you then have an instant meal or wonderful travel food for many days. Top them with tomatoes, sliced avocado and some sprouts and you may be surprised to hear yourself say, "Who needs cooked food?"

NO FANATICISM PLEASE!

I have seen many raw-foodists become so fanatic and rigid about eating only raw foods that it can actually take away from their health, both physically and emotionally. It has recently been shown that a diet of mostly raw foods with a lesser amount of cooked food is best for most people (there are always exceptions). What that ratio is varies for everyone and you will have to decide for yourself what feels right for you and your lifestyle. A bit of experimenting may be necessary to see what works best for you, and that will probably change with the seasons, your moods, and your own internal growth and change. I have found that my diet has evolved and changed, as I have evolved and changed in my life.

I believe it is also helpful to include some raw animal products from time to time, such as raw goat cheese or raw egg yolk (no egg white as it blocks the absorption of Biotin, a B vitamin). Their vitamin B 12 content is in a useable form that is hard to get from other sources.

CHANGING WITH THE SEASONS

It is natural, especially in colder climates, to crave more warm cooked foods in winter months. So it seems natural to me to eat more warm cooked foods during the winter. Baked yams, steamed vegetables, and warm soups are very nourishing on a cold winter day. There are wonderful recipes in this book for raw sauces you can use on steamed veggies or baked potatoes (be sure to let them cool a bit so you don't cook the sauce). In the summer, when it is too hot to cook and there are so many luscious, fresh fruits and vegetables available, you may want only raw foods for some months—it all balances out. If you want to eat more raw foods in the winter, but need something as warming as possible, try slightly warmed raw soups. The Sesame Squash Soup on page 99 is particularly good for colder winter days. You can also always add ginger to most recipes for a warming effect. The dehydrated "burgers" and loaves here are also very warming served right out of the dehydrator. Foods such as these can also be re-warmed (if they have gotten cold) in the dehydrator (110 degrees) just before serving.

GO ORGANIC!

In these recipes, organic ingredients are assumed. Buying and eating organic supports not only your body's health but the health of the planet.

BE CREATIVE!

My biggest piece of advice for live food preparation is to let your creative juices flow and don't be afraid to experiment. If you don't have a particular ingredient, substitute something else that you like. You may find you have a whole new creation you will want to write down and keep to be re-created another time. Don't be afraid of failure—it will happen from time to time, especially with big variations. At least then you know what *not* to do, which is just as important as knowing what to do! Use whatever is in season to achieve the best flavors. Add whatever herbs and spices you like best—everybody has their own favorites. I don't like spicy ingredients so I tend not to use hot peppers, but if you love that flavor, go for it!

Nuts and seeds are interchangeable in many recipes. Each has a slightly different flavor and texture, so experiment to find the combination you like best.

In some recipes calling for water, the milk from a young coconut can be used instead. It will add a sweet flavor and extra nutrition. Young coconuts are the ones that come encased in their outer white shell. The meat is tender and a wonderful addition to many recipes. You can also use the milk from a mature coconut.

MY STORY

In 1999, my health had slowly declined to such a degree that I sought out a doctor's help and advice, which I very rarely do. I tried my usual changes in diet, along with other natural methods of healing, but was still not feeling better. I was sleeping 12 hours a day, taking naps, and was still feeling exhausted all the time. Something clearly was not right. My holistic doctor, who diagnosed me with severe anemia, was aware that poor health can also sometimes be caused by what is happening in the mouth and sent me to see a holistic dentist. I was informed that the teeth on which I had root canals many years ago were probably infected and causing my health problems (not uncommon with root canals after many years) and should be extracted. After that horrendous procedure my health took a dramatic turn for the better and I began to feel alive again. As part of my health recovery and detox from my food addictions (see Chapter 7, Food and Emotions), I fasted for a week and then ate 100 percent live foods for a few months. It was during that time that I created many of these recipes (especially the desserts), as I was determined to make my meals delicious, unlike what I had thought in the past of live foods—boring, unsatisfying, too much work to chew, raw vegetables. I also had to make the meals relatively easy as I have never enjoyed spending hours in the kitchen every day.

While I was physically healing, I was introduced to Emotional Body Enlightenment (EBE) and started healing the emotional causes of so many health-threatening teeth problems. I'm certain I had been in danger of getting cancer as my dentist was amazed that I did not have breast cancer when he saw what was happening in my mouth—the infected teeth were directly on the meridian that also runs through the breasts. Most of the women he saw with as much mouth infections as I had, also had breast cancer. My mother had breast cancer which would have made it even more likely. I am certain I would not be here now if I had not discovered what was wrong and done my physical and emotional healing work.

Now, with the help of live food nutrition (I usually eat 50% to 90% raw, depending on the season) what foods are available where I am, and what I feel like eating, deep emotional healing, regular exercise, and Radiant Life Qigong, I feel more life-force in my body in my 50's than I did in my 20's and 30's. The body has huge regenerative powers and it is never too late to feel the benefits of a health-revealing lifestyle. I can tell you from personal experience that it is not necessary to lose life energy and strength just because the body reaches a certain chronological age. You won't become 20 again, but you can maximize the potential you do have.

CHAPTER 1
SOAKING, SPROUTING AND STORING

Dry nuts and seeds should be kept in a cool, dry place in a container that is inaccessible to insects (a tightly sealed glass jar is best), or preferably refrigerated, especially in summer months. They can also be frozen. Don't buy more shelled nuts than you will use in a year, as they will not keep forever. If you buy them in bulk, it is best to buy them in the fall, since they are freshest after the fall harvest.

Nuts and seeds should be soaked before eating to improve their ability to be digested and used by the body. Un-soaked, they contain a natural enzyme inhibitor that acts as a natural protection from decay until enough water comes in to enable them to sprout and start to grow. This enzyme inhibitor would typically be dissolved during the soaking process.

To soak nuts and seeds, put them in a jar and fill with filtered water. Make sure they stay covered, as they will swell and absorb some of the water. A general rule is to soak for at least 6 hours or overnight. There are many complicated soaking tables available (all with different soaking requirement times for the same nut) but, really 6 hours is enough and if you soak them a bit longer than required, no harm will be done. I believe in keeping it simple and not having to consult a chart every time you want to soak something.

Drain the water after soaking and the nuts are ready to use. When soaking flax and chia seeds, you will not be able to drain the water off them, so a 2:3 ratio of water to seeds is ideal for soaking these types as they will absorb all the water. After draining, the seeds will form a mucilaginous gel. Nuts with a very high fat content like Brazil nuts, pine nuts, and cashews do not need to be soaked. Hemp seeds do not need to be soaked, either.

Legumes and grains are not the ideal food for humans (they are hard to digest and have some natural toxins), but their occasional use is fine and you will find a few recipes here using them so I have included sprouting instructions for them also.

Always use filtered water for soaking and rinsing.

SIMPLE RULES FOR SOAKING AND SPROUTING

NUTS AND SEEDS

Soak all nuts and seeds in filtered water at least 6 hours or overnight and then drain well before use. Walnuts have a wonderful mellow flavor and are a great snack when soaked for 6 hours and then dehydrated until dry.

Soaking not required for:

- Brazil nuts
- Pine nuts
- Cashews
- Macadamia nuts
- Hemp seeds

LEGUMES AND GRAINS

When using garbanzo beans, lentils, quinoa, wheat/spelt berries, and oat groats, soak for 8 hours or overnight in a large jar. Drain water, lay the jar on its side, spreading out the seeds, and let them sprout in a dark place for about 16 hours, rinsing once or twice. Exact time will depend on how warm it is—they are ready when a tiny tail first appears. At that time they must be used immediately. However, if you need to wait a few hours, refrigeration will slow further sprouting. Rinse them before using.

Buckwheat groats should only be soaked for an hour or so and then drained and left to sprout, rinsing occasionally. Rinse again before using.

STORAGE

In general, nuts and seeds should be consumed shortly after soaking. Almonds are an exception as they will keep well for a week or so if you cover them in water in the refrigerator and change the water every day.

Soaked almonds can easily be peeled with the fingers and are a wonderful snack. The peel contains a natural toxin, so almonds are actually better eaten without the skin.

Keep in mind that most cashews sold in stores are not really raw. They have been heated in the process of removing them from their shells, which kills their enzymes. Truly raw cashews are available from raw food websites (see Sources on page 169).

> ❧ **A hint about nuts.** Soak nuts and dehydrate until dry again to have nuts on hand to avoid remembering to soak! This process especially mellows the taste of walnuts.
>
> ❧ **Grinding nuts.** There are various machines that will grind nuts, including the dry carafe of a Vitamix, a coffee grinder, and a food processor.

GENERAL FOOD STORAGE TIPS

Most raw foods are best prepared and eaten fresh for maximum life-force availability and nutrition. Some preparations will keep for a short time, however. All raw food should be stored in glass jars or covered glass bowls. Because the food is so alive, it can absorb molecules of any plastic (and aluminum, of course!) that it comes in contact with. Keep contact with plastic wraps to a minimum. The exception is dehydrated crackers—they can be stored in tightly sealed plastic containers (in a cool place) and will keep for a couple months, or longer.

Most fresh preparations will keep reasonably well for 1 day (in the refrigerator), if necessary. Tomato Sauce (see page 60) will keep for a week or so and Ketchup (see page 63) for a couple weeks.

Young coconut meat (removed from the shell) keeps well in the freezer and is handy to have in this ready-to-use form.

NOTE ON SALT

You will find that most of the recipes here use Krystal Salt brine. I recommend using only Krystal Salt (available from various websites and in many natural food stores) and keeping a jar of it on the kitchen counter at all times for ready use. To make the brine put 2 or 3 Krystal Salt rocks in a jar and fill with filtered water. After about 48 hours the salt will have dissolved to a 26% solution and after that will dissolve no more. Once all the salt is gone, you need to add more until some remains undissolved so you know the solution is saturated. If there are still rocks left, you can add more water as the level goes down. If you don't have Krystal Salt brine, you can use ¼ as much granulated Krystal salt.

MEASUREMENT NOTES

Measurements used here are before soaking. In other words, 1 cup almonds, soaked, means to measure them dry before they are soaked and then soak them. The soaked measure will, of course, be greater than the dry.

Measurement Conversions

SALT: 1 teaspoon Krystal Salt brine = ¼ teaspoon Krystal Salt granules

STEVIA: 1 teaspoon clear liquid concentrate = 1 teaspoon powder concentrate

CHAPTER 2
ABOUT DEHYDRATING

Some helpful tips and possible new ideas even for those who already have experience with dehydrating:

❧   **Flavors get more concentrated** in the drying process, so be careful when adding salt or other flavors—you may end up with an overly salty or strong-tasting finished product. It takes a bit of experimenting to find out what works for you to get the best results. The wet mixture should taste not quite salty and spicy enough to you.

❧   **Turning over.** Crackers, cookies, etc. started out on the Teflex sheets should be turned over and placed on the screens when they are dry enough to hold together. This will speed drying and make the drying more even.

❧   **Water content.** The less water you use when processing your crackers and cookies, the less time it will take to dehydrate them. This means more energy saved and less time for mold and bacteria to grow in the warm air. This may require more time spent stopping the food processor to scrape down the sides, but it will be worth the extra effort.

❧   **The temperature debate.** Low-temperature dehydrating warms and dries food without destroying all enzymes. Common knowledge is that enzymes are destroyed at temperatures above 118 degrees. That is coming into question however, as the research that this temperature was based on refers to an outside *water* temperature of 118, not the surrounding *air* temperature. What matters is what temperature the food reaches, not the air's temperature. The main problem is that there has been no real research done on this subject and no one really knows at what outside air temperature the food enzymes will be destroyed. Recent research by the Excalibur Dehydrator Company found that a higher than usual starting temperature will speed drying time and lessen the chance of mold and bacterial growth (the longer a food is exposed to warmth, the more potential for bacteria to grow), with no threat to enzyme health. The high water content of the food will keep it from actually reaching the initial drying temperature so enzymes are not in danger as long as you remember to turn the temperature down after the designated time. For a more complete explanation see Gabriel Cousen's book *The Secrets of Rainbow Green Live-Food Cuisine*. The Excalibur company recommends using a starting temperature of 145 degrees for 2 hours, depending on the water content of the food (very low water content foods, like bananas, should stay at that temperature for less time), then lowering to desired temperature for the duration of drying time. Because of the Excalibur fan system and precise temperature control, this is only recommended for the Excalibur dehydrators and not other brands.

CHAPTER 3

THE RAW KITCHEN

You can get by with just a basic blender if necessary, but there are some machines that can really make life easier and food preparing even more enjoyable. I would recommend obtaining as many of these items as you can afford. They last forever (well, a long time, anyway) and are worth the investment.

❧ A **Vitamix**, including the dry carafe, will blend anything with ease without fear of burning out the motor (it will shut itself off before it lets the motor burn up). The dry carafe will easily grind dry nuts and seeds for fudge and other recipes. It's a machine that doesn't seem necessary until you get one and then you don't know how you ever managed without it. It is a time saver too, as less chopping of ingredients is necessary. You can put in large chunks of almost any ingredient without a problem. Recipes that call for chopped items may need only quartering (or no chopping at all) with a Vitamix.

❧ **Coffee grinder**. Good for grinding a small amount of nuts, seeds, and raw cocoa beans.

❧ **Food processor**. Cuisinart makes an excellent food processor, but less expensive ones will work fine, too. They are also wonderful for grating and slicing large amounts. Look for one with an 8–10 cup capacity. Small ones for small amounts are also very useful.

❧ **Hand blender**. Great for blending small or larger amounts of some ingredients, and fairly inexpensive. Some come with a mini-food processor that is handy for small amounts and will also grind nuts. I highly recommend these items.

❧ **Dehydrator.** Excalibur is the best as the fan systems and temperature control prevents "hot spots" and keeps the food at an even temperature. It is also easy to use and clean. You will need the Teflex sheets also—if you are serious about raw foods, get the 9 tray size.

❧ **Juicer.** Green Star brand has magnetic technology that creates a very alive and nutrient-retaining juice. If you don't want to spend that much money, any triturating (Green Power, Green Star) or masticating (Champion, Omega) juicers do well and are capable of making nut butters and frozen desserts. Avoid centrifugal type juicers as they do not make a very good quality juice and are not as easy to use.

❧ **Ice Cream Maker.** They are fairly inexpensive and live food ice cream is such a wonderful treat! Any of the juicers recommended will also make ice cream out of frozen fruit, but with an ice cream maker you can make a more creamy version with nuts or seeds, egg yolk and whatever flavors you like (see Ice Cream section on page 161).

❧ A **Spiral Slicer** creates very thin "noodles" from hard squash for raw spaghetti, and the **Mandoline** makes veggie slices of various thicknesses with precision and ease.

❧ A **ceramic knife** will not cause oxidation from the food touching metal and does not need to be sharpened. They will chip rather easily, however, so slice carefully with them and do your chopping with other knives. Sharp, well-made knives (including metal ones) are a must, in my opinion, and are worth the investment. They make slicing and chopping so much easier and faster.

CHAPTER 4

IS IT REALLY RAW?

Let's review some common misconceptions about what is really raw and what is not.

Many store-bought products are labeled raw because they start with raw ingredients, but are then heated enough in their processing to no longer be considered truly raw.

If you use some ingredients that are not raw, it is not so important, but knowing what is really raw and what is not can be helpful in making an informed choice. I happen to prefer the "raw" carob powder that is not really raw. The truly raw one has a grainy taste and texture. I do recommend that foods with a high protein or fat content be raw whenever possible, as heated fat and protein has a completely different effect in the body than raw. Cooked proteins coagulate, making the amino acids difficult to be digested and used by the body. Heating fats can destroy their essential fatty acid content and actually turn healthy fats into harmful, or at the least unhealthy, ones. You are also much less likely to gain unwanted weight with raw fats than with cooked ones.

What is not raw even though it may be labeled raw:

❧ **Jarred nut and seed butters** that are not refrigerated. These are made with raw nuts and seeds so they can be labeled as raw, but they are either pasteurized or are exposed to too much heat in the grinding process, or both. In some locations it is possible to buy really raw nut butters but they will usually be sold in the refrigerated section and will be dated. If in doubt, ask the source.

❧   Most **cashews** are heated in the shelling process. Raw food websites sell really raw cashews.

❧   Most **raw milk cheeses** labeled as raw are heated over 120 degrees in the cheese making process, thereby killing the enzymes and making them no longer raw. Occasionally, some local producers of raw cheese (especially goat feta) do not heat their product, but the only way to know for sure is to ask the people who make it.

❧   Most **carob powder** labeled as raw is heated in the grinding process. Jaffe Bros mail order company has an unheated raw carob powder, as do other raw food mail order sources (see Sources on page 169).

❧   **Maple syrup** is used in some recipes here and in other raw recipe books, but it is definitely cooked.

What may or may not be raw:

❧   Commercial brands of **honey** are usually pasteurized but local brands are usually not, in my experience. If they sugar and get hard after awhile, this is a good sign, as they are probably not pasteurized. If they remain as liquid, they are probably pasteurized. Again, when in doubt, ask the producer.

❧   **Dried fruits** such as dates and raisins are often dried at too high a temperature to be raw. Raw food websites are a good source for finding these foods dried at low temperatures. Jaffe Bros is a good source of raw dates (see Sources on page 169).

❧   **Hemp seeds** may be irradiated when entering the United States. The company Manitoba Harvest, who packages them and sells them in most natural food stores, assures me theirs are not irradiated and are raw (see Sources on page 169).

CHAPTER 5
SIMPLE WAYS TO BOOST YOUR NUTRITION INTAKE

❧ **Add green leaves to your smoothies.** Romaine lettuce (or any dark leaved variety), chard, kale, collards, spinach (not too much because of the oxalic acid content), sunflower sprouts, buckwheat sprouts, parsley, celery, carrot tops, local wild edible greens, etc, along with your favorite fruits. Be sure to vary which greens you use. Making a green smoothie a part of your diet every day will help in many ways. Most of us do not chew well enough to get the maximum benefit from what we eat, especially greens. Blending greens helps to release the nutrients so they can be absorbed more efficiently by the body. What small amount is lost in oxidation will be more than made up for with digestibility. Green smoothies also increase the hydrochloric acid content of the stomach, which many of us have become deficient in, thereby leaving us open to various digestive problems and even parasites. Blended greens add more chlorophyll and amino acids to the diet and make the body alkaline. For a more detailed explanation of the value of green smoothies, read *Green for Life* by Victoria Boutenko. I personally recommend drinking a 5 Element Smoothie (see page 35) with green leaves added as your first meal of the day.

❧ **Juicing**. Make a vegetable juice of carrots, beets, and any green veggies listed above. You can also juice beet and turnip greens.

❧ **Take blue green algae from Klamath Lake**. It is the best supplement you can take because of its wide variety of hard to find important nutrients (EPA, DHA, B12, antioxidants, chlorophyll) in an easily assimilated form, and it is a wild food, therefore having the full life-force nature intended foods to have. Klamath Valley Botanicals produces a very high-quality algae.

❧ **Eat local wild edible greens**. Wild grown foods have the most life-force and nutrition of all plants. There are websites and books on this subject. Avoid plants growing next to busy streets.

❧ **Eat Goji berries.** These berries are antioxidants, minerals and vitamins packed in a small, easy to carry, tasty package.

❧ **Use Amazon Herb products.** These unique formulations with the life-force of the Amazon Rain Forest are very health supporting for the body.

A NOTE ON AMAZON HERBS

Amazon Herbs is a company that makes herbal formulations from the Amazon Rainforest that supports the body in creating and maintaining vibrant health in its natural de-toxing process. They are a wonderful, easy to use source of powerful antioxidants, among other things. Because the sources of these products are ancient rainforests that have been undisturbed for millennia, they contain a life-force most other supplements and herbal formulations do not have. The company has found a processing method that preserves nutrients in the best way possible, keeping this life-force alive. Using the products actually helps save the rainforests as native peoples in that area earn their living by ecologically maintaining and harvesting the forests to ensure their continuing health and productivity. The company also has a full skin care line that imparts this vibrant life-force to products for the face, which the skin then absorbs, resulting in a wonderful alive feeling. These products are made without chemicals or artificial preservatives and are of very high quality.

There are many reasons to experience these wonderful products. They also have a wonderful house cleaning product and products for pets. For more information (see Sources on page 169).

❧ **Use Krystal Salt** exclusively.

❧ **Drink a 5 Element Smoothie** (see page 35) as your first meal of the day (or any meal).

❧ **Eat organic**. Non-organic foods not only have chemical toxins on and in them (washing does not remove all chemicals), they have fewer nutrients because of the soil they are grown in, and are more likely to be hybrids or be genetically modified, which have fewer vitamins and minerals.

❧ **Get enough rest and exercise.** Exercise boosts the metabolism and is crucial for your body to obtain the energy needed to assimilate what you take in.

❧ **Take time to enjoy and appreciate your food**. Food eaten in a rush or with anxiety will not be assimilated as well as food eaten slowly with enjoyment and love.

CHAPTER 6
EATING ACCORDING TO OUR BIOLOGICAL DESIGN

The more foods we include in our diet that are what our bodies are biologically designed to eat (fresh, raw, organic fruits, vegetables, nuts and seeds), the easier it is for our bodies to be the radiantly healthy beings they were meant to be. This is not an edict to be strictly followed, but rather should be considered suggestions to move towards.

❧ Eat mostly fresh fruits, vegetables, soaked nuts and seeds and animal products, if desired. Minimize grain and legume intake.

❧ Eat foods that are as close to the way nature made them as possible. Processing, canning, over-cooking, etc. all take away nutrients and life-force.

❧ Include wild grown foods in your diet such as foods that grow naturally without having to be cultivated. Examples are Blue Green Algae (see page 24), wild edible plants, apples, pears, etc.

❧ When possible, eat non-hybridized fruits and vegetables, i.e. fruits with seeds. Seedless fruits are hybrids—nature needs its seeds to reproduce itself.

❧ Include as many raw leafy greens as possible.

❧ Include raw protein and fats from plant sources (soaked nuts and seeds). These proteins and fats are in a form that the body can easily make use of (because they are unaltered, the way nature made them) and are needed by the body for many functions. Flax seeds have the essential omega 3 fatty acids that so many bodies don't get enough of (see recipe for the 5 Element Smoothie on page 35).

❧ Drink purified water.

❧ Use Krystal Salt exclusively, it is the salt that is actually good for the body.

❧ Eat slowly, chew well, and do not eat when emotionally distressed.

CHAPTER 7
FOOD AND EMOTIONS

These two subjects are more deeply linked than most of us are aware. In this complicated world we live in, food has become more than just sustenance for the body. If that's all it was, we wouldn't be making many of the choices we do when it comes to our diets! Our bodies just do not have a natural physical requirement for chocolate (or many of the other things we eat), and I know of no disease brought on by the lack of it.

Just the thought of food can bring up powerful emotions and often childhood memories. Do you ever find yourself unable to stop eating a particular food that you know is not nourishing for your body, no matter how much willpower you employ? Or do you sometimes want to keep eating after your stomach says it is full, still feeling that something is not satisfied? It could be because you are looking for love or comfort in this food, not just physical nourishment (it could also indicate a real deficiency of a certain nutrient, but this is not often the case). The problem is that you cannot substitute food for love. You can eat until full and still not feel satisfied if unconscious emotional parts of you are actually looking for love.

Food is one of the most common substitutes for love and acceptance. In fact, it can even become an addiction we are unable or unwilling to go without. I'm not saying we should go without food, but we may need to examine our relationship with it.

PHYSIOLOGICALLY SPEAKING

There is a physiological reason for our connecting food with feelings. A mother who is breast-feeding undergoes neurological changes that increase her ability to feel emotions. Nature intended for us to combine the experience of receiving physical food with being felt emotionally. That is the healthy connection we are supposed to feel while nourishing our bodies physically. Unfortunately, mothers who have unhealed emotional congestions from their own childhood could have developed an emotional defense system that keeps them from feeling their children as deeply as the child needs to be. They are unconsciously withholding an emotional frequency of love and in that way are not letting the child fully love their mother (because love is about letting someone in, not about pouring love out). Children are then left with an unhealthy need for food as a way to get love. This is why taking away cherished food can be so very difficult for us. In adulthood we are not aware of the emotional being inside of us who needs the food, we only know we cannot do without that food. The next time you reach for that ice cream or chocolate, try feeling into what part of you is needing it, and why, and see what happens.

EQUATING FOOD WITH LOVE

There are also other contributions to the linking of food with emotions. Often there is too little love of any kind being expressed and felt in the family. We live busy and stressful lives with little time for allowing our feelings their full expression. Further deepening our love/food connection, stressed out parents often offer food as a substitute for not having "quality time" to spend with children. The food that parents offer them is sometimes the closest thing to love that children will feel. At least it is something coming from caregivers, even if it is not true nourishing love. Hence we learn another way to equate food with love. Another contribution to the lack of felt nourishment is eating food that is prepared under stress and hurriedness without love. Learning to overeat is the result of all this love starvation, with obvious consequences.

When food is used as a reward or punishment for children, emotional ties to the receiving or withholding of food are deepened even more. "If you're good, I'll let you have some cookies later." Or "Go to your room without dinner, that'll teach you to not talk back to me!" Or "Here is some ice cream, just stop screaming!" In other words, I don't want to or can't feel you right now so that you can know that I love you, so here is this food as a replacement to keep you from your feelings. Do any of these sound familiar? You probably have your own family versions of food being used as a reward or a pacifier, or the withholding of food as punishment. These are all ways we learn to create unhealthy relationships with food. Is it any wonder that the issue of what to eat can be so confusing as an adult, or that we have a need to give ourselves chocolate or ice cream to feel good about ourselves? Food becomes a way to cover up conscious or unconscious hurt. It is not surprising that such a high percentage of our population is overweight!

Emotional starvation is one reason why "diets" are doomed to fail. Parts of us get so emotionally starved from not having comfort foods, causing us to over-compensate when the diet is over and eat the same unhealthy foods to even greater excess to make up for the felt love starvation. Denying ourselves these foods is felt by those parts as taking away love, the love they didn't get in childhood and are still not getting now.

There is also often a deep feeling of unworthiness attached to food addictions. Parts of us, due to our childhood wounds, do not believe we deserve health! These feelings are usually unconscious to us and so we are not aware that our desire for unhealthy foods is just not a good thing, often driven by a deep-seated belief that we are not good enough to have vibrant health. So we choose foods that will sabotage our body's natural instinct for a state of well-being. Remember that health is not an absence of disease, but our natural state of vibrant energy and joy for life!

These are just some of the ways we learn to relate to food beyond the simple nourishment of the body and enjoyment of foods in the state nature created them. Food is not a bad thing for us, obviously, but sometimes our relationship to it needs to be examined and healed. Only then can we consciously make healthy food choices from a state of healthy self worth and self love, and not from needing to get love from something outside ourselves.

EMOTIONAL BODY ENLIGHTENMENT

There is an emotional healing process called Emotional Body Enlightenment (EBE) that heals the cause of our food addictions in addition to creating a deep sense of self worth. This helps us to learn a new, healthier way of eating and relating to food that is more in line with what our bodies actually need. The beauty of the EBE process is that it provides a map and a method to develop a relationship with those stuck, unconscious emotional parts and finally gives them the love and nourishment they have always craved. Emotionally healthy mothers are able to nourish their babies as nature intended and adults are no longer slaves to food cravings. I have seen in those practicing EBE that when emotional healing happens, cravings for things like chocolate and ice cream simply fall away because the formerly unconscious emotional parts are now getting the real thing. That doesn't mean those foods can't be enjoyed occasionally, it is just that they are not craved in an unhealthy way.

You can learn more about EBE at *www.theohumanity.org* and by reading *There's No Such Thing as a Negative Emotion* by Daniel Barron. EBE is mainly a spiritual work of learning how to inhabit, rather than transcend, our humanity. It is a challenging and rigorous process that is not for everyone, but can be life transmuting for those who are ready and willing to do whatever they can for their deepest healing.

ALL IN MODERATION

Most important of all is to not be rigid about what you eat, even (or especially) about eating raw foods. It has actually been proven healthier (for most people) to eat a mostly raw diet with some cooked foods than to eat only raw foods, although many raw foodists will vehemently deny this. Believe it or not, having an unhealthy relationship to raw foods is even possible! I recommend a widely varied diet in which you don't deny yourself a beloved food for the rest of your life just because it is "unhealthy". It is not so important what you eat once in a while, what matters is what you eat every day. Once you get yourself to a healed, authentic place emotionally, and away from junk food addictions that keep you stuck in unnatural food cravings, your body will tell you what it needs and what makes it feel good. Listen to it and use common sense.

CHAPTER 8

THE RECIPES

PART 1
THE 5 ELEMENT SMOOTHIE AND OTHER BREAKFAST FOODS

The body is still in cleansing mode in the morning and benefits most from a light meal at this time, rather than the usual heavy breakfast foods. Here are a few ideas to start your day with.

5 Element Smoothie

This recipe was created by Christian Opitz and is truly an amazingly alive, satisfying and energy-giving combination. A very complete meal indeed.

The combination of ingredients in the 5 Element Smoothie creates and enhances an electrical charge, which equates to more life-force, as we are electrical beings. Krystal Salt is a unique salt that contains all the elements of the human body woven into a crystalline structure that the body can easily use, unlike Celtic sea salt or other salts. It has a strong electrical force field (in and of itself) that enhances health and balances blood pressure. **Blue Green algae** is mineral-rich, power-packed nutrition with antioxidants, functional vitamin B12, plus the essential fatty acids EPA and DHA (important for brain function) and sulfuric amino acids, all of which combine to create an electrical charge/life-force our body needs to function. Adding the salt, flax seeds and lemon further enhances that charge. The combination of lemon and flax seeds is also a good liver cleanse. Try this as the first meal of your day and you may notice a difference in how you feel.

This smoothie balances the 5 elements/tastes according to Chinese medicine so all the ingredients are important. Here it is, the perfect meal:

Advance prep: 6 hours (or overnight) to soak flax seeds

½ small lemon, peeled (seeds and some of the white of the peel is acceptable)

a dash cayenne of or to taste (it is not necessary to be able to taste it)

½ teaspoon Krystal Salt brine (see note on page 37)

2 tablespoons flax seeds, soaked in about twice as much water overnight

water to blend

handful green leaves of your choice e.g. lettuce (dark green or red varieties), kale, chard, collards, spinach, celery, parsley, sunflower sprouts, local wild edible weeds, etc. If you are not used to the taste of green, start with just a couple leaves. Be sure to vary which leaves you use to avoid developing an intolerance to one type. Spinach should not be used every day because of the high oxalic acid content.

2–4 whole pieces sweet fruit (banana, pear, peach or whatever is in season). Using at least 1 banana or mango will give a nice creaminess.

Place all ingredients, except fruit, in blender. Blend very well. Add fruit and blend just until it is incorporated. Not blending the fruit too much will save some nutrients from oxidizing. It can also be blended all at once if you prefer. Take with Blue Green Algae on the side. This smoothie should be drank immediately. The Omega 3 fatty acids in flax seeds oxidize very quickly once they are ground.

To make salt brine, put chunks or crystals of Krystal Salt in water and let sit for about 48 hours. It will dissolve to a 26% solution at which point the salt will not dissolve any more. There should still be some salt left on the bottom so you know the solution is saturated. Serves 1.

1 tablespoon flax oil can be used instead of soaked flax seeds, if desired. Check pressing date of oil and only use within the first 6 weeks of pressing. This is very important, as flax oil must be fresh. Barleans is one of the best brands of flax oil.

Take Blue Green algae (using the recommended serving size on the bottle's label) at the same time when drinking the 5 Element Smoothie but do not add it to the smoothie.

Buckwheat Crunchies

Advance prep: 24 hours for soaking and sprouting plus 4–5 hours of dehydrating time.

2 cups raw buckwheat groats

Soak and sprout buckwheat groats for 24 hours. Drain well and dehydrate at 110 degrees 4 to 5 hours until crunchy. These are wonderful to keep handy in a jar for many uses. Serves 4.

Here are some variations:

- ❧   Add nut milk, honey, raisins, dates, banana, chopped nuts, etc for a quick breakfast (or snack) cereal.
- ❧   Add as a topping for salads or other dishes
- ❧   Use as a travel food

Mark's Oatmeal

Advance prep: Soak 6 hours and sprout oat groats (24 hours total prep), 6 hours for almonds

1 cup oat groats, soaked and sprouted
½ cup almonds, soaked
1 ripe banana, chopped
1 teaspoon Krystal Salt brine
¼ teaspoon cinnamon

Put banana in food processor first then add remaining ingredients. Process lightly until combined. Serve topped with raisins and/or soaked walnuts and honey, if desired. Serves 2.

As a variation, use cashews instead of almonds. The cashews do not need to be soaked. Buckwheat can be used instead of oat groats. Soak the buckwheat 1 hour then sprout for about 23 hours.

Crunchy Cereal

You can make a lot of this at one time and have ready-made cereal on hand. This is a basic recipe to which you can add other seeds or nuts, honey and/or dried fruit.

Advance prep: 24 hours soaking time plus about 4 hours dehydrating time

2 cups Buckwheat groats, soaked 1 hour, sprouted about 23 hours, drained well.
1 cup almonds, soaked, towel dried, and chopped (you can use a small food processor if desired)
1 teaspoon cinnamon
2 teaspoons Krystal salt brine

Combine ingredients well in a mixing bowl. Dehydrate on Teflex sheets at 110 degrees until crunchy. Serve with raisins and chopped banana or other fruit. Serves 6.

PART 2
BEVERAGES

Raw food beverages are not just something to drink with a meal, but also add valuable nutrition. They can also be a meal or snack by themselves.

Basic Milk Recipe

Advance prep: 6 hours to soak nuts or seeds

½ cup nuts or seeds, soaked (almonds or sunflower seeds
     work best)
2 cups water
sweetener of choice (honey, maple syrup, etc.)
1 teaspoon vanilla extract or any other flavoring (optional)

Place the soaked nuts or seeds in blender with 1 cup water. Blend for 1 minute on high speed. Add remaining ingredients and blend well. This can now be used as is if you don't mind a bit of pulp in it (it will be thicker and a bit grainy), or strain it through a straining cloth to remove the pulp for a more milk-like consistency (can be a fair amount of work). Serves 4.

Keeps in the refrigerator for a few days.

Use this recipe as a base for anything you need nut milk for, or just drink as is.

Luscious Hot Chocolate

Well, OK, it's really warm chocolate but is just as satisfying.

Advance prep: 6 hours to soak seeds or nuts

¼ cup sunflower seeds (or almonds), soaked
1¼ cups warm (not hot) water
3–5 dates
1 heaping tablespoon carob powder or raw cocoa powder
½ teaspoon vanilla
¼ teaspoon almond extract

First add seeds, dates and 1 cup water to blender and blend until smooth. Then add remaining ingredients and blend again until smooth. Warm slightly in a pan, if desired. Serves one.

Make sure the water is no more than 115 degrees or it will destroy the enzymes.

B&B Shake

The blueberries make this a very colorful drink.

Advance prep: 6 hours to soak sunflower seeds

2 cups Sunflower Milk (see basic milk recipe on page 41)
1 large banana
½ cup blueberries
3–5 dates or honey to taste

Blend well. Serves 2.

Mango Lassi

A raw version of this traditional Indian treat

Advance prep: none for cashews or 6 hours to soak almonds

2 cups Cashew or Almond Milk (see basic milk recipe on
　　　page 41)
2 mangos, peeled and pitted
½ teaspoon vanilla extract
2 tablespoons honey or to taste

Blend well. Serves 2.

Carob Banana Shake

*This idea is nothing new but is worth repeating because it is so good,
and so comforting.*

Advance prep: 6 hours to soak almonds

2 cups Almond Milk (see basic milk recipe on page 41)
2 ripe bananas
3–5 pitted dates
1 teaspoon vanilla extract
½ teaspoon almond extract

Combine all ingredients well in a blender and serve. More
almond milk (or water) may be needed if the bananas are very
big. Serves 2.

For a variation, try adding a few strawberries.

Strawberry Delight

This is a summer treat as the strawberries and almonds make a refreshing combination.

Advance prep: 6 hours to soak almonds

2 cups Almond Milk (see basic milk recipe on page 41)
1 cup strawberries
¼ cup dates

Blend well. Serves 2.

Tropical Shake

This decadent drink is sure to take you to the shores of Hawaii in your imagination.

Advance prep: none

1 cup Macadamia Nut Milk (see basic milk recipe on
          page 41)
1 cup young coconut milk
meat from 1 young coconut
1 cup pineapple chunks

Combine all ingredients well in blender and serve topped with grated coconut. Serves 2.

Green Smoothies

A very tasty way to get greens and the benefits of their chlorophyll and other nutrients into the body. The blending of these greens makes their nutrient value more easily assimilated by the body. Use a variety of greens including kale, collards, parsley, Swiss chard, Romaine or red leaf lettuce (or any deep green/red variety), sprouts, celery, spinach, carrot tops, local edible wild weeds such as chickweed, miner's lettuce, purslane, lamb's quarters, stinging nettles, etc.

One example:

1 apple, cored and chopped
1 pear, cored and chopped
½ bunch kale
1 stalk celery
water to blend

Place everything in blender and blend well.

The idea is to combine any of your favorite fruits that are in season with any of the above greens. Ideally you will have at least one large handful of greens per serving, with one or two whole pieces of fruit, plus water to blend. Be sure to rotate which greens you use and don't use the same one each time. Remember, we need variety!

PART 3
DRESSINGS

A daily salad is an important part of any diet, and in a live food program they certainly can be a very filling meal themselves. These dressings are a big part of a salad's satisfying nature as they contain nuts, seeds and vegetables. A variety of dressing ideas to choose from is essential to keep salads from being boring! Remember, these are just suggestions to get you started—experiment with whatever flavors you most enjoy.

You can always make a simple and delicious salad dressing with olive oil, lemon juice, crushed garlic and dried or fresh herbs of your choice, but it is not necessary to use oil to have a wonderful dressing. The dressings here are all rich and creamy using whole nuts and seeds instead of oils. I like to use a lot of dressing on my salads for a very filling meal.

Almond Cheese Dressing

Advance prep: 6 hours to soak almonds

½ cup almonds, soaked
¼ cup raw goat feta cheese
1 medium red or yellow bell pepper
1 teaspoon Krystal Salt brine
½ clove garlic
water to blend

Blend all ingredients until smooth adding enough water for desired consistency. Makes 2–3 large salads.

Avocado Dressing

Advance prep: 6 hours to soak seeds

1 avocado
2 tablespoons sunflower seeds, soaked
1 tablespoon tahini
¼ cup chopped sweet onion or 1 tablespoon yellow onion
2 teaspoons Krystal Salt brine
water to blend to desired consistency

Blend all to a creamy consistency. Makes 2 large or 4 small salads.

Cream of Corn Dressing

This makes a very creamy dressing

Advance prep: none

½ cup pine nuts
2 ears corn, cut off cob
½ avocado
¼ cup chopped onion
½ cup chopped tomato
1 clove garlic
1 teaspoon Krystal Salt brine
water to blend to desired consistency

Blend well and pour generously over salad. Makes 2–3 large salads.

Creamy Dill Dressing

Advance prep: none

½ cup pine nuts
⅓ cup water
2 tablespoons lemon juice
1 bunch fresh dill
½ teaspoon garlic
Krystal Salt brine to taste

Blend well and pour over your favorite salad greens. Makes 2 large salads.

Pesto Dressing

Advance prep: none

2 large tomatoes or red bell peppers, chopped
⅓ cup packed fresh basil
½ cup pine nuts
2 tablespoons miso
1 clove garlic
1 tablespoon raw goat feta (optional)
water to blend, if bell peppers are used

Blend all well in blender. Makes 2–3 large salads.

Pine Nut Dressing/Sauce

Rich and creamy, this one will please everyone!

Advance prep: none or 6 hours to soak almonds

1 cup pine nuts (or ½ cup pine nuts, ½ cup soaked
      almonds)
1 large red bell pepper
1 tablespoon miso
1 clove garlic
1 teaspoon Krystal Salt brine
pinch of cayenne (optional)
water to blend to desired consistency

Blend all in blender to smooth consistency. Makes 3–4 large
salads. Also makes a good sauce.

Shiitake Dressing

Advance prep: none or 6 hours to soak nuts or seeds

2 large red bell peppers
1 medium to large carrot
½ cup soaked sunflower seeds, almonds and/or avocado
1½ tablespoons miso
1 clove garlic
2–3 Shiitake mushrooms
water

Chop vegetables if necessary and blend all well with enough water for desired consistency. Goes great with a spinach, tomato and alfalfa sprout salad. Also makes a nice soup. Makes 2 large salads.

> Sunflower seeds, almonds, pumpkin seeds and avocado all work well in this recipe. Use one or a combination.

Summer Dressing

Make this in the summer when corn and sweet onions are available. It is a wonderful combination of sweet and savory.

Advance prep: none

4 medium tomatoes
2 ears corn, cut off cob
¼ cup pine nuts
½ cup chopped sweet onion (or to taste)
¼ cup fresh basil
2–3 teaspoons Krystal Salt brine

Blend all well and pour generously over your favorite salad. Makes 2–3 large salads.

Tahini Lemon Dressing

This is a simple classic dressing that is very easy to make.

Advance prep: none

½ cup water
3 tablespoons tahini, or ¼ cup sesame seeds
1 tablespoon lemon juice
1 tablespoon Nama Shoyu
1 teaspoon chopped garlic

Blend until smooth and creamy in a blender. Makes about ¾ cup.

Tomato Avocado Dressing

Advance prep: 6 hours to soak nuts or seeds

2 large tomatoes, quartered
1 ripe avocado
¼ cup almonds or sunflower seeds, soaked
1 tablespoon miso
1 clove crushed garlic
¼ teaspoon Italian Blend dried herbs
water to blend to desired consistency

Blend all ingredients well. Makes 2–3 large salads.

Tomato Shiitake Dressing

Advance prep: 6 hours to soak sunflower seeds

2 medium tomatoes
2 shiitake mushrooms
½ cup soaked sunflower seeds
2 tablespoons raw goat cheese
1 tablespoon miso
½ teaspoon Krystal Salt brine
1 clove garlic
¼ teaspoon Italian blend dried herbs
¼ cup water

Blend well and pour over your favorite greens. Makes 2 large salads.

PART 4
SAUCES AND GRAVIES

A good sauce can make anything taste good! Use them to top chopped or grated veggies or dehydrated veggie/nut patties. If you are not all raw, they make great toppings for baked potatoes and steamed vegetables (a wonderful warming winter meal).

Almond Goat Feta Sauce

This sauce will make you feel like you are in a 5 star restaurant

Advance prep: 6 hours to soak almonds

½ cup almonds, soaked
½ cup crumbled goat feta cheese
½ to 1 clove garlic
1 teaspoon Krystal Salt brine, or to taste
pinch of thyme
pinch marjoram
water

Place all ingredients in blender and blend until smooth, adding enough water for desired consistency. Taste and adjust seasonings, if desired. Serve over raw (or steamed) veggies. Serves 4.

As a variation, try substituting ½ or all almonds with pine nuts.

Lemon Sauce

Here is an idea for what to do with fresh raw asparagus.

Advance prep: 6 hours to soak sunflower seeds

½ cup sunflower seeds, soaked
Juice of ½ lemon (about 4 tablespoons)
1 raw egg yolk (optional)
2 teaspoons Krystal Salt brine
½ clove garlic
¼ teaspoon dried dill
¼ teaspoon dried tarragon
1 bunch asparagus, tough bottoms removed

Blend all ingredients, except the asparagus, well in blender. Make a bed of lettuce, place chopped asparagus on top and drizzle the sauce over asparagus and lettuce. Serves 3–4.

Seedy Cheese Sauce

This and the Almond Goat Feta Sauce (page 55) are so much better than any cooked cheese sauce ever was, in my humble opinion!

Advance prep: 6 hours to soak seeds

½ cup sunflower seeds, soaked
¼ cup pumpkin seeds, soaked
⅓ cup raw goat cheese, crumbled
½ cup chopped tomatoes
1 teaspoon vegetable broth powder
1 teaspoon Krystal Salt brine or to taste
1 teaspoon Nama Shoyu or to taste
½ to 1 clove garlic
pinch of thyme
pinch of marjoram
water

Put all ingredients in a blender and blend until smooth, adding enough water for desired consistency. Adjust seasonings, if desired. It is hard to recommend exact amounts of salty items to use as the salt content of goat cheese varies, as does vegetable broth powder. Serves 4 or more.

Use left-over sauce on crackers or breads as a spread.

Nut Veggie sauce

Advance prep: 6 hours to soak nuts

½ cup almonds, soaked
½ cup cashews
1 medium zucchini
½ red or yellow bell pepper, seeded
1–2 tablespoons onion, sweet variety if available
2 teaspoons Krystal Salt brine, or to taste

Place veggies in blender first, then add remaining ingredients. Blend well, adding a small amount of water, if necessary. Serves 4.

Simple Sauce

Advance prep: 6 hours to soak nuts

½ cup almonds, soaked
½ cup walnuts, soaked
1 tablespoon onion, chopped
2 teaspoons Krystal Salt brine
water to blend to desired consistency

Blend well in blender. Serves 4.

Spicy Seed Sauce

Advance prep: 6 hours to soak seeds

½ cup sunflower seeds, soaked
½ cup pumpkin seeds, soaked
1 tablespoon onion, chopped
1 clove garlic
2 teaspoons Krystal Salt Brine
¼ teaspoon dried marjoram
¼ teaspoon dried basil
pinch of cayenne pepper
water to blend to desired consistency

Blend all ingredients well in blender or small food processor.
Serves 4.

Holiday Sauce

A sweet and spicy sauce for special occasions and cold winter days.

Advance prep: 6 hours to soak nuts

1 cup pecans, soaked
1 tablespoon maple syrup or honey
½ teaspoon Krystal Salt brine
¼ teaspoon cinnamon
pinch cloves and/or nutmeg
water to blend

Blend all ingredients well, adding water as necessary for desired consistency. Serve over grated yams or squash. Serves 4.

Tomato Sauce

Advance prep: 20 minutes to soak dried tomatoes

2 cups tomatoes, chopped
½ cup dried tomatoes, soaked
¼ cup fresh basil leaves or 1 teaspoon dried
¼ cup fresh oregano or 1 teaspoon dried
¼ cup red or white wine (or water)
5 pitted raw olives
juice of ½ lemon
½ teaspoon peeled, chopped ginger
1 clove garlic
3 teaspoons Krystal Salt brine

Soak dried tomatoes 20 minutes in just enough water to cover. Place all ingredients in blender including tomato soak water and blend until well combined. Store left-over sauce in a glass jar in refrigerator. Keeps for a week or so. Makes about 3 cups.

Makes a great sauce for pizza, nut loaves or patties, or use as a cracker topping.

Gravy

This raw version is amazingly tasty.

Advance prep: none

¼ cup pine nuts
¼ cup miso
juice of ½ orange (or at least ¼ cup)
¼ cup chopped leek or onion
1 clove garlic
2 medium dates
1 tablespoon wine, red or white
1 tablespoon raw tahini or sesame seeds
½ teaspoon chopped, peeled ginger
water to blend

Combine all ingredients in blender until creamy, adding enough water for desired consistency. Serve over Mashed Cauliflower "Potatoes" (page 128), veggies or dehydrated "burgers", "meatballs", etc. Makes 1½ to 2 cups.

Cashew Corn Gravy

This is as yummy as it sounds!

Advance prep: none

½ cup cashews
1 ear corn, cut off cob
1 tablespoon chopped onion
1 teaspoon Krystal Salt brine
¼ teaspoon vegetable broth powder
¼ cup water

Blend all until creamy. Serve over meatloaf. Serves 2.

Ketchup

There is no need to do without this classic favorite in raw cuisine. Amazingly better than the cooked version.

Advance prep: 20 minutes to soak dried tomatoes

1 cup fresh tomatoes, chopped
1 cup dried tomatoes, soaked
¼ cup onion, chopped
¼ cup packed, pitted dates
¼ cup maple syrup
1 tablespoon fresh ginger, peeled and sliced
1 tablespoon fresh basil leaves, packed (or ½ teaspoon
    dried)
1 clove garlic, chopped
1 teaspoon Krystal Salt granules
water to blend

Place dried tomatoes in just enough water to cover while preparing other ingredients. Blend all ingredients well in a blender, including tomato soak water, adding a bit of water if necessary, but only enough for it to turn over. It will thicken up more after blending is completed. Keeps up to 2 weeks in the refrigerator. Use on dehydrated burgers, meatloaf or crackers. Serves 6.

Pesto

Always a classic and useful in so many ways.

Advance prep: none

½ red bell pepper
3 bunches basil, stems removed
½ cup pine nuts
1 clove garlic, chopped
¼ cup raw goat cheese, crumbled or 2 tablespoons miso
Krystal Salt or more miso to taste
olive oil to blend

Immerse basil in basin of water to wash, lifting out of water to drain. Dry well. Add ingredients to food processor in order listed. Process, scraping down as necessary to incorporate all ingredients, adding only enough olive oil to make a thick paste. Serves 6.

Spread on dehydrated crackers and top with veggies for a great "pizza".

PART 5
SALADS

These salads with nut or seed-based dressings can make a very satisfying meal by themselves, or can be served as a side dish. Be creative! If you don't have a particular vegetable in your refrigerator, use whatever you have.

Arame Sprout Salad

This makes a lot of dressing but don't be afraid to use it all to make almost a salad/soup. It really adds to the flavor and makes the salad quite filling.

Advance prep: 6 hours to soak seeds, 20 minutes to soak Arame

1 large handful sunflower or other sprouts
½ cup dry Arame seaweed, soaked
Shiitake or Portobello mushrooms, thinly sliced
1 large carrot, finely grated

Dressing:
1 large red or yellow bell pepper
¼–½ cup sunflower or pumpkin seeds, soaked (use ½ cup
    for two people)
1 heaping tablespoon miso
½ clove garlic or to taste
basil or Italian Seasoning to taste
½ avocado (optional)
water to blend

Soak Arame in water to cover 15–20 minutes, then drain. Blend all dressing ingredients until smooth. In a large bowl, mix salad ingredients with dressing and enjoy. Serves one as a meal or two smaller salads.

Asparagus Cauliflower Crunch

Advance prep: pre-prepared Pâté, or 6 hours to soak seeds

Salad:
1 cup cauliflower, chopped into small pieces
1 cup asparagus, chopped into 1 inch lengths
⅓ cup carrots, thinly sliced with a Mandoline
¼ cup shelled peas

Sauce/dressing:
1 large tomato
½ cup of any type of pâté, or soaked sunflower or pumpkin
    seeds
1 avocado
¼ cup raw goat cheese
1 teaspoon broth powder
Kyrstal Salt brine and Nama Shoyu to taste
water to blend

Place vegetables in a large bowl. Blend sauce ingredients well and pour over vegetables. Mix well. There should be enough sauce for all veggies to be well covered. Makes 2 large servings.

Asparagus Salad

Advance prep: Lemon Sauce (see page 56)

1 bunch asparagus
lettuce leaves
Lemon Sauce

Snap off tough ends of asparagus and use them for juicing. Wash and chop the rest into bite size pieces. Place on top of lettuce leaves and top with Lemon Sauce. Serves 2.

Avo Tomato Cucumber Salad

This combination has a wonderful flavor, takes only a few minutes to prepare, and only requires one bowl to make, saving clean up time!

Advance prep: none

2 large tomatoes, chopped
2 cups sliced cucumber
2 ears corn, cut off cob
1 avocado
1 cup ground cherries (optional, but really good if you can
        get them)
¼ cup crumbled raw goat feta
1 clove pressed garlic
½ teaspoon Vegit or other dried veggie/herb combo
1 teaspoon Krystal Salt brine

Mash avocado into bottom of large bowl. Add remaining ingredients and mix well. Serves 2.

Blended Salads

Although not for the faint at heart (blended greens definitely taste, well, green), this type of salad is easy to prepare and easy to digest. Most people don't chew their food well enough to get maximum nutrition from it (and after many years of dental work it may be just not possible any more) and blending the greens makes the nutrients more readily accessible. The whole salad can be blended, but I find that adding some grated veggies to the blend satisfies that need to chew.

Advance prep: 6 hours to soak nuts or seeds

To blend:
¼–½ cup soaked nuts or seeds of your choice
1 med to large fresh tomato
One or two large handfuls salad greens of your choice
1 stalk celery
Slice fresh garlic
Krystal Salt brine to taste
Pinch Italian Seasoning or ½ teaspoon broth powder
Nama Shoyu to taste (optional)

Salad:
Grated carrots
Grated zucchini or other summer squash
Grated beets
Grated or chopped jicama
Shelled English peas
Chopped sugar snap peas

Place first set of ingredients in blender and pour over second set of ingredients. Top with grated raw goat cheese, if desired. Serve with crackers topped with avocado or raw goat cheese. Serves 1.

Cinnamon Holiday Salad

Sweet and cinnamon-y, this salad is an easy to make addition to the holiday buffet.

Advance prep: 2 hours to soak raisins

1 cup finely grated winter squash
1 cup finely grated kohlrabi
½ cup finely grated carrots
½ cup raisins, soaked in water to cover at least 2 hours
2 tablespoons olive oil
½ teaspoon Krystal Salt brine
cinnamon to taste

Combine all ingredients except raisin soak water and serve chilled. You can add some of the raisin soak water at the end if you like a really sweet salad. Serves 4–6.

Creamy Cucumber Tomato Salad

This is one of my favorite summer salads as it is so simple. The taste of cucumber and tomato goes together so well.

Advance prep: none

Place in bowl:
3 large tomatoes, chopped
3 cucumbers, sliced
1 cup raw pitted olives, sliced in half

Dressing:
½ cup raw cashews
¼ cup raw goat feta or avocado
1 clove garlic
½ teaspoon Krystal Salt brine
1 teaspoon miso

Blend dressing ingredients in blender until smooth. Pour over salad ingredients and stir well. Makes 2 fairly large salads.

Green Vibrance Salad

The key to this salad is to slice the kale very thin—the thinner it is the more tender it gets in the marinating process. You can use a variety of added vegetables, depending on what is in season.

Advance prep: 24 hours to soak and sprout lentils or 6 hours to soak sun seeds, 3–4 hours marinating time

Salad:

1 bunch kale (Lancelate variety is best) very thinly sliced

¾ cup lentils (or sunflower seeds, soaked), soaked and
        sprouted 24 hours

1 large red bell pepper, chopped

2 tablespoons fresh chives or ¼ cup green onion, chopped

1 or 2 ears fresh corn, cut off cob, or 1 bunch asparagus,
        chopped or 2 chopped tomatoes

Marinade:

¼ cup raw dates

¼ cup raw tahini* or sesame seeds

juice of 2 oranges

juice of ½ lemon

1 tablespoon olive oil

2 teaspoons Nama Shoyu

1 or 2 cloves garlic (to taste)

½ teaspoon Italian Blend dried herbs

*Note: If raw tahini is not available (most "raw" butters sold in jars are not raw), put ¼ cup dry sesame seeds in the blender first and grind to a powder before adding the remaining marinade ingredients.

Blend marinade ingredients until smooth. Pour over salad ingredients and mix well. Refrigerate 3–4 hours, stirring occasionally, before serving.

Serve topped with chopped walnuts, pecans, or soaked sunflower seeds. Serves 2–4.

Quick Salad

Here is an idea for when you are hungry and want something fast to fix. It also is a use for that pâté you have in the refrigerator.

Advance prep: pre-prepared pâté, dehydrated crackers

Any leftover vegetables

Chop into small pieces whatever veggies you have in the refrigerator, such as cauliflower, asparagus, broccoli, zucchini, tomatoes, peas, etc. Top with a large spoonful or two of pâté and mix well. Served with a few dehydrated crackers topped with sprouts, it is a satisfying, quick and easy meal. Serves one.

Ratatouille

Advance prep: 6 hours to soak pumpkin seeds, pre-prepared Tomato Sauce, 2 or more hours marinating time

2 medium zucchini, chopped
2 medium tomatoes, chopped
2 ears corn, cut off cob
2 portobello mushrooms, chopped
½ cup chopped onion, preferably sweet variety
2 cups Tomato Sauce (see page 60)
½ cup pumpkin seeds, soaked
2 teaspoons Krystal Salt brine
1 tablespoon lemon juice
¼ teaspoon dried basil (or ¼ cup fresh, chopped)
¼ teaspoon Italian Blend seasoning
small pinch of thyme
avocado

Combine all ingredients well (except avocado) and let marinate, refrigerated, for 2 or more hours. Stir occasionally during the marinating time. Serve on a bed of lettuce topped with avocado slices. Serves 3–4.

Note: If you don't have tomato sauce already prepared and are in a hurry, you can marinate the Ratatouille in blended fresh tomatoes with a bit of salt added.

Savory Cucumber Tomato Salad
Super easy—only one bowl and no blending required

Advance prep: none

2 medium cucumbers, sliced
1½ cups chopped tomato
½ cup sunflower seeds, soaked
¼ cup crumbled raw goat feta
1 teaspoon Krystal Salt brine
1½ teaspoons Vegit seasoning
1 clove garlic, pressed

Combine all in a large bowl. Serves 2.

Shiitake-Seaweed Blended Salad

The taste of the Shiitakes really comes through in this surprisingly good-tasting blended salad. The Arame adds another distinct flavor.

Advance prep: 6 hours to soak sunflower seeds

½ cup sunflower seeds, soaked
1 large red bell pepper, chopped
2–3 cups spinach, packed
4 romaine lettuce leaves, torn into pieces
6 medium Shiitake mushrooms
2 tablespoons goat cheese (optional)
2 teaspoons Krystal Salt brine
Nama Shoyu to taste
1 clove garlic
dash of marjoram
dash of basil
water to blend

Add to salad after blending:
alfalfa sprouts
soaked Arame

Place about ½ cup Arame in a bowl and cover with water to soak. Place salad ingredients in Vitamix and blend well. You may need to push down the greens to get them to incorporate. Pour into two bowls and add drained Arame. Top with sprouts. Serves 2–3.

Spinach Carrot Salad with Walnut/ Tomato Crème

This is a decadent, rich tasting salad.

Advance prep: 6 hours to soak walnuts, 10–20 minutes to soak dried tomatoes

Salad:
Baby spinach leaves (enough for two people)
2 medium carrots, grated

Dressing:
½ avocado
¼ cup walnuts, soaked
¼ cup dried tomatoes, soaked 10–20 minutes
slice garlic (or to taste)
dash of Italian Blend seasoning
1 teaspoon Nama Shoyu
1 teaspoon lemon juice
Krystal Salt to taste
water to blend

Blend dressing ingredients (including tomato soak water) in Vitamix to a thick, coarse consistency. It is best if the dried tomatoes don't get completely blended. Pour over spinach and carrots and mix well. Makes two large salads.

Spinach Cauliflower Salad
A salad with an Indian flavor

Advance prep: 6 hours to soak almonds, 2 or more hours to marinate

Salad:
1 head cauliflower, chopped fine
3 cups spinach, chopped fine
8–10 mushrooms of choice, chopped

Dressing:
juice of one orange
juice of 1 lemon
½ cup almonds, soaked
1 red bell pepper, chopped
¼ cup raisins
1 teaspoon garam masala
4 teaspoons Krystal Salt brine

Combine dressing ingredients in blender and pour over salad ingredients. Marinate in refrigerator for 2 or more hours before serving. Serves 4–6.

"Tuna" Salad

Looks a bit like green tuna salad but tastes much better!

Advance prep: 24 hours to soak and sprout lentils, 6 hours to soak sunflower seeds, 15 minutes to soak Arame

2 small avocados
½ cup sunflower seeds, soaked
1 teaspoon Krystal Salt brine
1 teaspoon Nama Shoyu or to taste
3 small carrots, grated fine
½ cup dry Arame, soaked 15 minutes
½ cup lentils, soaked and sprouted about 24 hours
1 cup chopped, peeled jicama
lettuce and/or green sprouts
water to blend

Place avocado, sunflower seeds, brine and Nama Shoyu in blender. Blend well, adding only enough water to make a thick sauce.

In a large bowl, combine blended mixture with carrots, drained Arame, lentils and jicama. Serve over bed of lettuce, mixed salad greens and/or sprouts. Serves 2–3.

Winter salad

This salad is sweet and savory

Advance prep: 2 hours to soak raisins

½ cup finely grated winter squash
½ cup finely grated kohlrabi
½ cup finely grated red beets
½ cup finely grated carrots
⅓ cup raisins, soaked at least 2 hours
2 tablespoons olive oil
1 teaspoon lemon juice
½ to 1 teaspoon Krystal Salt brine
½ clove pressed garlic

Stir all ingredients together well except the raisin soak water. Add some raisin soak water at the end if you want a slightly sweeter salad. Serves 4.

PART 6
DEHYDRATED CRACKERS

Each of these recipes takes only an hour or two time investment to yield many instant meals.

It is recommended that you either double the recipes or make more than one at a time to fill your dehydrator and make full use of dehydrating time (and the electricity needed). One of the dehydrated cookie recipes (see Dessert, page 141) can also help fill it.

Corn Chips
So much better than the cooked ones!

Advance prep: 6 hours to soak sun seeds or none for cashews, dehydrating time

5 large ears corn, cut off cob
1 cup raw cashews (best), or sunflower seeds, soaked
2 teaspoons Krystal Salt brine
2 or more teaspoons Nama Shoyu

Process all in a food processor for 4 or 5 minutes until it is very smooth. Drop by spoonfuls onto Teflex sheets then shake the screens to flatten slightly. Dehydrate at 145 degrees (60°C) for 2 hours then at 110 degrees (45°C) until crispy. When they are dry enough to hold together, turn them over and place on screen to speed drying. Makes about 20 crackers.

Curry Crackers

These are a nice spicy vegetable cracker. The list of ingredients looks long but they really don't take much time to make.

Advance prep: 6 hours to soak seeds, dehydrating time

1 cup sunflower seeds, soaked
1 cup pumpkin seeds, soaked
½ cup un-hulled sesame seeds, soaked
1 cup chopped tomatoes
⅓ cup chopped green beans
⅓ cup chopped red bell pepper
1 tablespoon chopped onion
1 clove garlic
2 teaspoons Krystal Salt brine
3 teaspoons Nama Shoyu
2 teaspoons curry powder
½ teaspoon turmeric
cayenne power to taste (optional)
½ teaspoon vegetable broth powder or Vegit

Place tomatoes and beans in processor first then add remaining ingredients. Process to desired consistency. Drop by spoonfuls onto Teflex sheets and flatten to about ½ inch thick. Dehydrate for 2 hours at 145 degrees, then at 110 degrees until dry. Turn them over when they will hold together, and place on screens to speed drying time.

As a variation, add ¼ teaspoon ginger juice. To make juice, finely grate fresh ginger and squeeze out juice from pulp.

Pumpernickel Cookies

These don't taste anything at all like pumpernickel, but have that same dark, chewy texture to them. A little sweet, they are halfway between a cracker and a cookie.

Advance prep: 2 hours to soak raisins, 6 hours to soak seeds, about 18 hours for the quinoa, dehydrating time

1 cup quinoa, soaked and sprouted
1 cup pumpkin seeds, soaked
2 bananas
½ cup soaked raisins (just enough water to cover)
1 teaspoon Krystal Salt brine
1 teaspoon cinnamon

Blend everything (including raisin soak water) but one banana in a food processor. When mixture is smooth enough, stir in another chopped banana, but don't blend. Drop by spoons-full onto Teflex sheets and flatten slightly. Dehydrate for 2 hours at 145 degrees (60°C) then at 110 degrees (45°C) until chewy. When they are dry enough to hold together, turn them over and place on screen to speed drying. Makes about 20 cookies.

> As a variation, try adding ⅓ to ½ cup carob powder.

Quinoa Sesame Crackers

Advance prep: about 18 hours to soak and sprout quinoa, 6 hours for seeds, dehydrating time

1 cup quinoa, soaked and sprouted
1 cup sesame seeds, soaked
1 teaspoon chopped garlic
1½ tablespoons Nama Shoyu
1 teaspoon Krystal Salt brine

Process all until smooth. Drop by spoonfulls onto Teflex sheets and flatten to ½ inch thick. Dehydrate for 2 hours at 145 degrees (60°C) then at 110 degrees (45°C) until chewy or crispy as desired. When they are dry enough to hold together, turn them over and place on screen to speed drying. Makes about 18 crackers.

As a variation, add a handful of pine nuts and some tomatoes or a couple tablespoons grated parmesan cheese.

Vegi-Seed Crackers

A nice combination of different seeds and vegetables.

Advance prep: 6 hours to soak seeds and nuts, dehydrating time

1¼ cups flax seed, soaked in 2 cups water
¾ cup almonds, soaked
¾ cup sunflower seeds, soaked
1 medium zucchini, sliced
½ red or yellow bell pepper, chopped
2 small carrots, chopped
1 teaspoon Krystal Salt brine
1 small clove garlic
¼ teaspoon dried basil
½ teaspoon dried marjoram
3½ teaspoons Nama Shoyu

Combine all ingredients in food processor and process until everything is well ground and blended. Spread into ¼ inch thick rounds on Teflex sheets of dehydrator. Dehydrate for 2 hours at 145 degrees (60°C) then, at 110 degrees (45°C) until crispy. When they are dry enough to hold together, turn them over and place on screen to speed drying. Makes about 24 crackers.

Sun Crackers

These are tender and tasty.

Advance prep: 6 hours for soaking, dehydrating time

1 cup sunflower seeds, soaked
1 cup almonds, soaked
1 large red, yellow or orange bell pepper, chopped
1 large carrot, chopped
2 heaping tablespoons chopped onion
3 teaspoons Nama Shoyu, or to taste
1 teaspoon Krystal Salt brine

Place all ingredients in food processor and process until smooth. You will need to keep pushing everything down and scraping the sides from time to time. If necessary, add a bit of water. Drop by spoonfuls onto Teflex sheets of dehydrator and flatten into ¼ inch thick rounds. Dehydrate for 2 hours at 145 degrees (60°C) then at 110 degrees (45°C) until dry and crispy. When they are dry enough to hold together, turn them over and place on screen to speed drying. Makes about 18 crackers.

Vegetable Crackers

These make a great travel food or instant meal topped with avocado, sliced tomato and sprouts.

Advance prep: 6 hours for soaking, dehydrating time

1 cup almonds, soaked
1 cup flax seeds, soaked in 2 cups water
1 large red, yellow or orange bell pepper, chopped
3 small carrots, chopped
1 stalk celery, chopped
3 teaspoons Nama Shoyu or to taste
1 teaspoon Krystal Salt brine
1 clove garlic, chopped
¼ teaspoon dried basil
pinch dried marjoram

Place all ingredients in food processor and process until smooth. You will need to keep pushing everything down and scraping the sides from time to time. Drop by spoonfuls onto Teflex sheets of the dehydrator and flatten into ¼–½ inch thick rounds. Dehydrate at 145 degrees (60°C) for 2 hours, then at 110 degrees (45°C) until dry and crispy. When they are dry enough to hold together, turn them over and place on screen to speed drying. Makes about 18 crackers.

Yam Crackers

Chewy and a bit sweet with a slight smoky flavor from the pumpkin seeds, these will quickly become a family favorite!

Advance prep: 6 hours for soaking, dehydrating time

2 medium yams, grated
1 cup pumpkin seeds, soaked
½ large red bell pepper, chopped
¼ cup water plus 2 tablespoons
1 teaspoon Krystal Salt brine
1½ teaspoons Nama Shoyu, or to taste

Grate yams with grating blade of food processor. Place all ingredients in food processor and process until well combined and blended, scraping down sides from time to time. Drop by spoonfuls onto Teflex sheets of dehydrator and flatten into ¼ inch thick small rounds. Dehydrate for 2 hours at 145 degrees (60°C) then at 110 degrees (45°C) until chewy but not completely dry. When they are dry enough to hold together, turn them over and place on screen to speed drying. Makes about 18 crackers.

Buckwheat Pizza Crackers

Advance prep: 24 hours to soak and sprout buckwheat, 6 hours to soak sunflower seeds, dehydrating time

1 cup buckwheat, soaked and sprouted until a small tail emerges
1 cup sunflower seeds, soaked
1 cup chopped tomato
1–2 tablespoons chopped onion
4 teaspoons Krystal Salt brine
1½ teaspoons dried Italian Blend herbs

Place tomato in food processor first. Then follow with remaining ingredients, draining off excess water from buckwheat first. Process until smooth. Spread onto Teflex sheets ¼ to ½ inch (1 cm) thick and 4 to 5 inches (10–13 cm) across. Dehydrate at 145 degrees (60°C) for 2 hours then at 110 degrees (45°C) to desired dryness. When they are dry enough to hold together, turn them over and place on screen to speed drying. Makes about 10 crackers.

Flax Pizza Crackers

These are very simple to make.

Advance prep: 6 hours to soak flax seeds, dehydrating time

2 cups flax seeds, soaked in 4 cups water
4 medium tomatoes, chopped
¼ cup chopped onion
1 teaspoon Krystal salt crystals
1 teaspoon Italian blend herbs
½ teaspoon dried oregano

In food processor, blend all ingredients until tomatoes and onion are well combined. Flax seeds will stay whole. Spread into 4 inch rounds on Teflex sheets of dehydrator, ¼ to ½ inch (1 cm) thick and dehydrate for 2 hours at 145 degrees (60°C) then at 110 degrees (45°C) until crispy. When they are dry enough to hold together, turn them over and place on screen to speed drying. Makes about 10 crackers.

Seed Pizza Crackers

These are one of the best tasting pizza crackers I have ever had.

Advance prep: 6 hours to soak seeds, dehydrating time

1 cup pumpkin seeds, soaked
1 cup sunflower seeds, soaked
1 large zucchini, sliced
1 stalk celery, chopped
2 tablespoons chopped onion
1 teaspoon Italian Blend herbs
½ teaspoon oregano
½ teaspoon Kyrstal Salt granules

Process all until well combined in food processor. Spread onto Teflex sheets into 4 to 5 inch (10-13 cm) rounds ½ inch (1 cm) thick. Dehydrate for 2 hours at 145 degrees (60°C) then at 110 degrees (45°C) until dry. When they are dry enough to hold together, turn them over and place on screen to speed drying. Makes about 8 crackers.

PART 7
SOUPS

Raw soups can actually be quite versatile and not taste "raw" at all. Add less water and you have a wonderful sauce or salad dressing. In the winter they can be warmed slightly (not over 115 degrees) and so serve that desire for something warming when it is cold outside. A good way to safely warm them is to warm the bowls before adding the soup or place the bowl of soup in a pan or sink of hot water for a few minutes.

Serve with some dehydrated crackers and a salad for a complete meal.

ITEMS THAT MAKE GOOD SOUP

Here are some suggestions to make your own soup combinations:

Vegetables:

- Red or yellow bell pepper
- Tomato
- Corn
- Carrots
- Winter squash
- Spinach

Fat/Proteins:

- Any soaked nuts or seeds (pine nuts and cashews don't need to be soaked), especially sunflower seeds, almonds, pumpkin seeds, cashews, and pine nuts.
- Avocado
- Raw goat cheese

FLAVORINGS:

- Miso
- Garlic
- Onion
- Ginger
- Hot peppers
- Any spices/herbs you like
- Sliced mushrooms and soaked Arame make a nice garnish

The trick is to find the right combination of vegetables, foods containing fat, and seasonings for your taste. Experimenting is fun!

Corn Bell Pepper Soup

Sweet, simple and tasty!

Advance prep: none or 6 hours to soak nuts or seeds

2 ears corn, cut off cob
2 large red bell peppers
½ cup almonds or sunflower seeds, soaked or 1 avocado
2 teaspoons miso
½ clove garlic
young coconut milk or water to blend

Blend well, adding water to desired thickness. Serves 2.

Golden Sun Soup

So yummy you may be temped to have it for dessert!

Advance prep: 6 hours to soak almonds

2 ears corn, cut off cob
2 large yellow bell peppers, seeded, cut into large pieces
½ cup almonds, soaked
meat of 1 young coconut
1 tablespoon sweet onion, chopped
2 teaspoons miso
½ clove garlic
young coconut milk to blend

Place ingredients in order listed into blender and blend well.
Serves 2 as a main dish or 4 as a side dish.

Ginger Butternut Soup

The ginger makes this a warming soup in winter

Advance prep: none

2 cups chopped, peeled Butternut squash
½ cup chopped carrot
½ cup raw cashews
1 tablespoon mild flavored miso
½–1 teaspoon Krystal Salt brine
½–1 clove garlic
½ teaspoon chopped ginger, or to taste
water to blend

Put all ingredients in Vitamix or blender with enough water to blend to desired consistency. Serve in pre-warmed bowls. Serves 2.

Shiitake Seaweed Soup

Advance prep: none or 6 hours to soak seeds

2 large red bell peppers, chopped
2 small carrots, chopped
2 tablespoons mild flavored miso
1 clove garlic
½ cup sunflower seeds, soaked or 1 avocado
¾ cup Arame, soaked in water 10 minutes.
8–10 Shiitake mushrooms, stems removed and chopped

Put bell pepper, carrot, miso, garlic and seeds or avocado into blender. Add just enough water for desired soup consistency and blend well. Pour into pre-warmed bowls, add drained Arame and chopped mushrooms and stir. Serves 2–3.

Sesame Squash Soup

A wonderful soup that is as good as any cooked version!

Advance prep: 6 hours to soak sesame seeds, 20 minutes to soak dried tomatoes

2½ cups chopped, peeled winter squash
½ cup sesame seeds, soaked
⅓ cup dried tomatoes, soaked
⅓ cup chopped red bell pepper
1 tablespoon honey
1 medium clove garlic
½ teaspoon peeled ginger
1 teaspoon vegetable broth powder
¼ teaspoon herb salt or herb combo without salt
2 teaspoons Krystal Salt brine
Nama Shoyu to taste
water to blend

Start soaking tomatoes while you add remaining ingredients to blender. Add all ingredients (including tomato soak water) to Vitamix and blend until smooth and slightly warm. Serve slightly warmed in pre-warmed bowls. You can warm the bowls by filling them with hot water for a few minutes. Serves 3.

If you don't have a Vitamix, be careful not to burn the motor of your blender with this recipe. You may need to do half at a time and it might not come out as smooth.

As a variation, add fresh peas, mashed avocado and/or soaked Arame to the soup after blending.

Shiitake Soup

Sunflower seeds, almonds, pumpkin seeds and avocado all work well in this recipe. Use one or a combination.

Advance prep: none or 6 hours to soak seeds or nuts

2 large red bell peppers
½ cup soaked sunflower seeds, almonds and/or avocado
1 medium to large carrot
1½ tablespoons miso
1 clove garlic
2–3 Shiitake mushrooms
water to blend

Chop vegetables as necessary for your blender. Blend all ingredients well with enough water for desired consistency. Serve in pre-warmed bowls. Serves 2.

Tomato Olive Soup

The avocado gives it a nice thickness. Use heirloom tomatoes for the best taste.

Advance prep: 6 hours to soak seeds

4 medium tomatoes
½ avocado
¼ cup sunflower seeds, soaked
1 tablespoon chopped onion, sweet variety is best
1 tablespoon mild flavored miso
2 teaspoons Krystal Salt brine, or to taste
¼ teaspoon Italian Blend seasoning
chopped olives

Blend all well in blender except olives. Divide into bowls and top with chopped olives. Serve with dehydrated crackers. Serves 2.

Tomato Soup

This is a simple one without a lot of ingredients required. Use heirloom tomatoes for the best taste. Great summer soup.

Advance prep: 6 hours to soak seeds

3 medium tomatoes
¼ cup sunflower seeds, soaked
1 ear corn, cut off cob
¼ large red bell pepper
1 tablespoon chopped onion, sweet variety is best
1 tablespoon miso
1 teaspoon Krystal Salt brine, or to taste
Italian Blend seasoning to taste

Blend all well in blender. Serves 2.

PART 8
RAW DAIRY

It is possible to get a very cheesy taste with only nuts and seeds. These recipes can be a good substitute for those who want to avoid animal products completely, or a good addition to small amounts of raw milk cheeses.

Almond Ricotta

Slightly sweet—you will get raves when you serve this. It makes a wonderful dip for vegetables.

Advance prep: 6 hours to soak almonds

1⅓ cups almonds, soaked
1½ medium carrots, chopped
1 clove garlic
3 teaspoons Nama Shoyu
½ teaspoon lemon juice
½ teaspoon dried tarragon or thyme
¼ teaspoon dried oregano
young coconut milk or 2 dates

Put all ingredients in blender or food processor with just enough coconut milk or water to allow it to turn over. Process until smooth. Use as a dip for zucchini, cauliflower, carrots, etc., or as a spread for crackers. Can be used as a salad dressing by adding more water. Makes about 2 cups.

Pizza Cheese

This is very rich and nicely replaces cheese on raw pizzas.

Advance prep: 20 minutes to soak dried tomatoes

1 cup macadamia nuts
1 cup pine nuts
1 medium tomato
⅓ cup dried tomatoes soaked in just enough water to cover
⅓ cup chopped onion
1 tablespoon lemon juice
1 teaspoon Krystal Salt granules
1 teaspoon dried basil
1 teaspoon dried oregano

Put tomatoes in the food processor first (including dried tomato soak water) then add remaining ingredients. Process until smooth, scraping down sides when necessary. Spread on pizza crackers with tomato sauce and top with your favorite veggies. Makes about 3½ cups.

Cheese Topping

This can be used for pizzas, dehydrated crackers, sliced veggies, etc. Will keep for several days in the refrigerator.

Advance prep: 6 hours to soak almonds, 20 minutes to soak dried tomatoes

½ cup almonds, soaked
½ cup cashews
⅔ cup dried tomatoes soaked in ⅔ cup water for 20 minutes
½ teaspoon Italian Blend dried herbs
¼ teaspoon dried oregano or 1 teaspoon fresh
1 tablespoon Krystal Salt brine, or to taste
water to blend

Place all ingredients in blender or small food processer and blend until smooth, adding only as much water as necessary to blend or process. Makes about 1¾ cups.

PART 9
PÂTÉS

WHAT TO DO WITH PÂTÉS

A bowl of pâté in the refrigerator is useful for so many things. Just don't make more than you will use in a couple days as it will not keep long. The addition of garlic and lemon juice acts as a preservative if you are not going to eat it all immediately. Here are some suggestions for pâté uses:

- Spread on sliced Portobello mushrooms, zucchini, dried eggplant, cucumbers, bell peppers, tomatoes, etc.
- Use as a dip for veggies or crackers.
- Use as a spread for crackers and breads (baked or raw).
- Add water and blend for a salad dressing or sauce for raw or steamed veggies.
- Topping for cooked potatoes (let potatoes cool a bit first so they don't cook the pâté). Much better than sour cream.
- Add broth powder, onion and water and blend for a gravy.
- Make raw sushi with nori and veggie strips.

A Simple Pâté

This is a basic recipe and from here you can make many variations.

Advance prep: 6 hours to soak seeds

1 large red or yellow bell pepper, chopped
1 cup sunflower seeds, soaked
1 cup pumpkin seeds, soaked
1 or more garlic cloves, chopped
1 tablespoon lemon juice
1 teaspoon Krystal Salt brine
1 tablespoon Nama Shoyu or to taste
fresh or dried basil to taste

Add ingredients in order listed to food processor. Process until smooth, scraping down sides as necessary. You may need to add a little water, but only enough so it will turn over. Makes about 3 cups pâté.

Use to make sushi with vegetable strips rolled up in nori sheets, or as a spread on dehydrated crackers or breads. Can be used as a salad dressing if thinned with water.

Corn Almond Pâté

The fresh corn adds a bit of sweetness and compliments the nuts and seeds well.

Advance prep: 6 hours to soak nuts and seeds

1 cup almonds, soaked
1 cup sunflower seeds, soaked
1 large red bell pepper, chopped
1 ear fresh corn, cut off cob
1 tablespoon chopped onion
1 large clove garlic
1 tablespoon lemon juice
1 teaspoon Krystal Salt brine
1 tablespoon Nama Shoyu or to taste
½ teaspoon Italian Blend dried herbs
Water to blend

Place bell pepper and corn in food processor first then add remaining ingredients and process until smooth. Add only enough water to allow the ingredients to turn over. You will need to scrape down the sides fairly often. Makes about 3 cups.

Green Pea Pâté

This was inspired out of an abundance of peas in the garden and it worked!

Advance prep: 6 hours to soak seeds

1 cup sunflower seeds, soaked
1 cup pumpkin seeds, soaked
½ cup shelled fresh peas
¼ cup packed fresh basil leaves
1 tablespoon lemon juice
1 teaspoon Krystal Salt brine
1 tablespoon Nama Shoyu or to taste
1 clove garlic
1 tablespoon chopped fresh arugula (optional)

Process all ingredients in food processor to smooth consistency, adding only enough water for it to turn over. You will need to keep scraping the sides down. Makes about 3 cups pâté.

Jicama Pâté

Another version of the ever versatile raw pâté

Advance prep: 6 hours to soak nuts and seeds

¾ cup raw cashews, soaked or un-soaked
¾ cup sunflower seeds, soaked
¾ cup jicama
¼ cup young coconut milk
2 tablespoons raw goat cheese
1 tablespoon miso
1 teaspoon lemon juice
1 teaspoon Krystal Salt brine
½ clove garlic, chopped

Drain soaked cashews and sunflower seeds well and put in food processor along with the remaining ingredients. Process until smooth. Great as a dip for sliced veggie such as bell pepper, zucchini, celery, jicama, Portobello mushrooms, etc. Makes about 3 cups pâté.

Olive Tomato Pâté

This pâté has a hint of a Mediterranean flavor

Advance prep: 6 hours to soak nuts and seeds

1 cup sunflower seeds, soaked
1 cup almonds, soaked
1 large tomato, chopped
⅓ cup ripe olives, pitted
1 tablespoon Nama Shoyu, or to taste
1 tablespoon lemon juice
1 clove garlic, chopped
½ teaspoon Italian Blend dried herbs

Put the chopped tomato in the food processor first, then add the remaining ingredients. Process until smooth, adding just enough water for it to turn over. You will need to scrape the sides down occasionally. Taste and add more soy sauce if desired. Makes about 3 cups.

Pineapple Pâté

An unusual and flavorful pâté!

Advance prep: 6 hours to soak nuts and seeds

¾ cup cashews, soaked
¾ cup sunflower seeds, soaked
¾ cup chopped pineapple
¼ cup young coconut milk
2 tablespoons raw goat cheese (optional)
1 tablespoon mild flavored miso
1 tablespoon lemon juice
1 teaspoon Krystal Salt brine
½ clove garlic, chopped

Drain soaked cashews and sunflower seeds well and put in food processor along with the remaining ingredients. Process until smooth. Great as a dip for sliced veggie such as, bell pepper, zucchini, celery, jicama, Portobello mushrooms, etc. Makes about 3¼ cups.

Winter Pâté

This pâté is good in winter when other veggies like bell peppers are not available or are too expensive.

Advance prep: 6 hours to soak seeds

1 cup sunflower seeds, soaked
½ cup pumpkin seeds, soaked
½ cup chopped hard winter squash
¼ cup chopped carrots
¼ cup leeks, sliced
1 tablespoon lemon juice
1 clove garlic, chopped
2 or more teaspoons Nama Shoyu
1 teaspoon Krystal Salt brine
¼ teaspoon dried thyme or to taste

Process everything in a food processor until smooth, slowly adding just enough water for it to turn over. You will need to keep scraping sides down. Taste and adjust seasonings if desired. Makes 2½ cups pâté.

Vegetable Spread

A pâté variation but with more veggies

Advance prep: 6 hours to soak nuts

1 cup soaked almonds, well drained and patted dry
2 medium red or yellow bell peppers, chopped
1 large carrot, grated
1 stalk celery, chopped
2 tablespoons mild flavored miso
1 clove garlic, chopped
1 teaspoon lemon juice
¼ teaspoon dried tarragon
¼ teaspoon dried oregano
Nama Shoyu to taste

Process all in food processor to smooth consistency. Serve on crackers or as a dip for sliced veggie such as, bell pepper, zucchini, celery, jicama, Portobello mushrooms. Makes about 2½ cups.

PART 10
SIDES AND HEARTY CREATIONS

These recipes can be served as a main dish, or in smaller portions as a side dish. They are more dense—and more filling—recipes that will leave even raw food sceptics with a new experience.

'Bello Burger
Moist and meaty, these will amaze you!

Advance prep: 6 hours to soak nuts, dehydrating time

1 cup almonds, soaked
½ large red bell pepper, chopped
2 medium Portobello mushroom caps, chopped
1 small carrot, cut into ½ inch slices
2 tablespoons onion, chopped
1 small clove garlic
1½ tablespoons mild flavored miso
1 teaspoon lemon juice
¼ teaspoon dried basil

Process all in food processor to smooth consistency. You will need to keep scraping down the sides and may need to add a couple tablespoons water, but be careful not to add too much. Drop by ¼ cups-full onto Teflex sheets and form into patties about ¾ inch thick. Dehydrate 2 hours at 145 degrees, then about 1½ hours at 110 degrees to moist burger consistency. Serve warm from dehydrator. Makes 12 small patties.

> Serve with your favorite sauce or ketchup and sliced tomatoes. They will keep for a day in the refrigerator if necessary.

Savory Neat Balls

Serve these and you will feel like a raw gourmet!

Advance prep: 6 hours to soak nuts, dehydrating time

1 cup almonds, soaked
¾ cup walnuts, soaked
1 stalk chopped celery
¼ cup sliced leeks
¼ cup chopped carrot
1½ teaspoons Krystal Salt brine
2 teaspoons Nama Shoyu, or to taste
pinch of sage or to taste
pinch of thyme or to taste

Put vegetables in food processor then add the remaining ingredients. Process, adding a bit of water to help it turn over, if necessary. Be careful to add only a bit of water—you will need to keep scraping down the sides for it to all incorporate. If there is too much liquid, you will not be able to form balls. Form into 1½ inch balls and dehydrate at 145 degrees for 1 hour. If they are not dry enough, continue dehydrating at 110 degrees until they have a slight crust on the outside but are soft on the inside, 1 or 2 hours more.

Serve warm, fresh from the dehydrator, with Tomato Sauce (see page 60). Makes about 23 balls, serving 3–4.

Cauliflower Cream Curry

This is really good with young coconut milk, but water will work, too.

Advance prep: 24 hours to soak and sprout garbanzo beans, 6 hours to soak nuts and seeds

Place in large bowl:

2 cups cauliflower, chopped into small pieces

1 cup chopped spinach, packed

¼ cup dry garbanzo beans (chickpeas), soaked and sprouted until a tiny tail appears (about 24 hours)

Sauce:

½ cup un-hulled sesame seeds, soaked

½ cup walnuts, soaked

1 medium tomato, chopped

1 clove garlic

3 teaspoons Krystal Salt brine

2 teaspoons curry powder, or to taste

½ teaspoon garam masala

pinch cayenne powder (optional)

water or young coconut milk to blend to thick sauce

Blend sauce well in blender and pour over cauliflower, garbanzo beans and spinach. Mix well. Serves 3–4 as a main dish. Can be marinated in refrigerator for several hours.

Eggplant Ratatouille

Advance prep: 6 hours to soak seeds, 20 minutes to soak dried tomatoes

2 small eggplants, grated
2 small zucchini, grated
¼ cup chopped olives

Sauce:
2 small tomatoes
1 red bell pepper
½ cup soaked pumpkin seeds, drained
⅓ cup dried tomatoes, soaked in ⅓ cup water 20 minutes
¼ teaspoon Italian blend dried herbs
¼ teaspoon garlic
1 tablespoon Krystal salt brine, or to taste

In blender blend all sauce ingredients (including tomato soak water) well. Add a little water, if necessary, but you want a thick sauce. Combine eggplant, zucchini and olives. Divide into individual bowls and pour sauce over. Serves 3–4.

Portobello Pizza

A tasty and simple pizza

Advance prep: 6 hours to soak almond, 20 minutes to soak dried tomatoes

Crust:
2 Portobello mushrooms, sliced ¼ inch thick

Cheese:
¼ cup almonds, soaked
¼ cup cashews
⅓ cup dried tomatoes soaked in ⅓ cup water for 20 minutes
¼ teaspoon Italian Blend dried herbs
pinch of oregano
2 teaspoons Krystal Salt brine, or to taste

Topping:
1 large avocado, peeled and seeded
2 cups spinach, packed
1 teaspoon Krystal Salt brine
1 tablespoon onion, chopped
pinch oregano

Combine cheese ingredients, including tomato soak water, in small food processor and process using pulses until smooth. You may need to add a little water, but you want a thick cheese. Taste and add more salt, if desired.

Put topping ingredients in small bowl and blend with hand blender until smooth.

Assemble pizza by placing a layer of cheese on mushroom slice and top with avocado spinach mixture. Can also be served as an hor d'eurve if cut into bite size pieces. Serves 2 as a main course.

Holiday Yams (or squash)

Advance prep: None

½ large yam, grated per person, or 1 cup grated butternut
squash
Holiday Sauce (see page 59)

Top grated yams or squash with sauce for a side dish.
Serves 1.

Mary's Falafel

There are lots of raw Falafel recipes out there—this is my version. It does require some advance planning but is worth the effort for a special dinner.

Advance prep: 1½ days. Start soaking the garbanzo beans and sunflower seeds the first morning. Drain them in the evening and put in a dark place to continue sprouting. Rinse them again before using the next morning. The second morning start dehydrating and you will have warm Falafel that evening.

1¼ cups garbanzo beans (chickpeas), soaked and sprouted
        24 hours
1 cup sunflower seeds, soaked and sprouted
¼ cup tahini or ⅓ cup ground sesame seeds
3 tablespoons lemon juice
2 heaping tablespoons chopped onion
2 tablespoons packed fresh cilantro
4 teaspoons Nama Shoyu
1 tablespoon packed fresh parsley
1 tablespoon Krystal Salt brine
1 clove garlic, chopped
1½ teaspoons curry powder
½ teaspoon cumin
water

Place everything in a food processor and process well, adding only enough water for it to barely turn over, if necessary. You will need to keep scraping the sides down. Form into round or elongated patties about 1 inch thick and place on Teflex sheets of dehydrator. Dehydrate at 145 degrees for 2 hours, then lower temperature to 110 degrees and dehydrate about 4½ hours more. Turn them over and place on screens when they will hold together. They are done when they have a crust on the outside but are moist on the inside. Makes 8–10 patties.

Great topped with avocado and served with asparagus and lemon sauce.

Guacamole and Chips

Another raw version of a favorite Mexican classic

Advance prep: Corn Chips recipe

Corn Chips (see page 81)
2 cups avocado
½ cup finely chopped tomato
¼ cup onion or green onion, chopped fine
¼ cup fresh cilantro, chopped fine
1 tablespoon lemon or lime juice
½ to 1 teaspoon Krystal Salt granules
chopped jalapeno to taste (optional)

In a mixing bowl mash avocado well with a fork. Stir in remaining ingredients. Use as a dip for corn chips and/or veggies. Another idea is to wrap Guacamole in cabbage or lettuce leaves. Makes about 3 cups of guacamole.

Little Sandwiches

Here is an idea for a simple snack or lunch

Advance prep: Crackers recipe

Crackers, any kind
Tomatoes, sliced
Avocado, sliced
Green sprouts, any kind
1 teaspoon Nama Shoyu mixed with 1 teaspoon water

Top your favorite cracker with the above ingredients. Dip in Nama Shoyu mix. Quick, simple and tasty! Serves 1.

Swiss Chard Rolls

Young, tender leaves are best for this.

Advance prep: 6 hours to soak almonds

½ cup almonds, soaked
1 cup chopped, peeled Kohlrabi
1 teaspoon lemon juice
herb salt to taste
¼ teaspoon dried thyme
water to blend
4–6 large green leaves (Swiss Chard or lettuce can be used)
handful of fresh shelled peas (optional)

Process almonds, Kohlrabi, herb salt and thyme in food processor until smooth. Add if bit of water if necessary, but be careful to not add too much. You will need to keep scraping down the sides. Place a large spoonful of the mixture at the base of a leaf and spread out to the width. Add a few fresh peas, if desired. Roll from base of leaf and secure with tooth pick. Makes 4–6 rolls.

These are even better the second day after a night in the refrigerator, so don't be afraid to double or triple this recipe.

If smaller rolls are desired you can cut the leaves in quarters and make smaller finger food sized rolls.

Mashed Cauliflower "Potatoes"

This simpler version was inspired by a recipe from Juliano's book Raw, this is wonderful covered with Gravy (see page 61).

Advance prep: Gravy recipe

3 cups chopped cauliflower
1 cup cashews (or half cashews and half pine nuts)
Juice of 1 lemon
1 tablespoon mild flavored miso
2 teaspoons Nama Shoyu, or to taste
1 clove garlic
¼ teaspoon dried thyme

Place all ingredients in food processor and process until very smooth. If necessary, add a tiny bit of water, but you will need to keep scraping the sides down. Serves 4 as a side dish.

Veggie Loaf

This is a very satisfying and tasty meal and a good combination of vegetables, nuts and seeds.

Advance prep: 6 hours to soak sunflower seeds, dehydrating time

1 medium zucchini, sliced
1 medium carrot, sliced
1 medium yellow or red bell pepper, chopped
½ cup sunflower seeds, soaked and well drained
½ cup pecans or walnuts not soaked, or soaked and dried
¼ cup pine nuts
1 tablespoon chopped onion
⅛ teaspoon Krystal Salt granules
2 teaspoons Nama Shoyu
¼ teaspoon dried tarragon
½ teaspoon dried basil or 7 large fresh leaves

Place all ingredients, in the order listed, in food processor and process until smooth. You will need to scrape the sides down once or twice. For a firmer loaf consistency form into 3 or 4 loaves on Teflex sheets and dehydrate at 145 degrees for 2 hours, then at 110 degrees about 2 hours more. It will be moist on the inside with a slight crust on the outside. Can also be eaten as is, without dehydrating. Serve on a bed of lettuce and sprouts and top with Cashew Corn Gravy (page 62) or Tomato Sauce (page 60). Serves 3–4 as a main dish.

Nori Rolls

These can be a meal in themselves or served as an appetizer

Advance prep: pre-prepared Pâté

nori sheets, not toasted
Pâté, any type
Veggies such as, carrots, zucchini (cut in strips), avocado,
    sprouts

On the dull side of the nori sheet place a strip of pâté and veggies, close to one end. Roll up as tightly as possible. Seal the
end by dabbing water on it. Slice into 1 inch thick rounds, if
desired. Makes one serving per sheet of nori.

Pizza

There are lots of recipes for raw pizza—here are a few more varieties to choose from. Worth the effort for a special feast.

Advance prep: Pizza Crackers, Tomato Sauce, Pizza Cheese, Pesto recipes

Pizza Crackers (see pages 89–91 for different variations)
Tomato Sauce (see page 60)
Pizza Cheese (see page 104)
Pesto (see page 49)

Toppings:
chopped veggies of choice e.g. mushrooms, zucchini, red
bell pepper, olives, onions, etc.

Layer tomato sauce and pizza cheese, or pesto only, on pizza crackers. Top with your favorite toppings and enjoy a feast.

Dream Wraps

I recommend serving these sausage-like rolls with a lot of lettuce leaves as they are a very dense food.

Advance prep: 6 hours to soak seeds, dehydrating time

¾ cup almonds, un-soaked or soaked and dehydrated
¼ cup pumpkin seeds, soaked
¼ cup pine nuts
½ large avocado
1 medium carrot, grated fine
¾ teaspoon fresh ginger, chopped
1 tablespoon fresh parsley
4 teaspoons Krystal Salt brine
1 tablespoon fresh sage or ½ teaspoon dried
½ tablespoon fresh thyme or ¼ teaspoon dried
Romaine lettuce leaves

Grind almonds to a powder in dry carafe of Vitamix. (If you use freshly soaked almonds, there will be too much moisture to form the rolls.) Place pumpkin seeds, pine nuts, avocado, ginger, salt, parsley and herbs in small food processor and process until smooth. Grate carrots into a large bowl. Add processor mixture and almonds, stir well. Check seasonings and adjust, if desired. Form into 1 inch diameter by about 4 inch long, sausage-like rolls and place on Teflex dehydrator sheets. Dehydrate for 1 hour at 145 degrees, then turn them over and place on screens for 1 to 2 hours at 110 degrees. Wrap them in lettuce leaves with Ketchup or a tiny bit of prepared mustard, if desired. Makes about 9 rolls.

Shiitake Burgers

Hearty and filling, these will satisfy any appetite.

Advance prep: 24 hours to soak and sprout garbanzo beans, 6 hours to soak sunflower seeds, dehydrating time

6 or 7 Shiitake mushrooms

2 tablespoons Nama Shoyu

1 tablespoon olive oil

1 cup garbanzo beans, soaked and sprouted (about 24 hours)

¾ cup sunflower seeds, soaked

½ cup raw tahini

¼ cup chopped onion

1 clove chopped garlic

curry powder and cumin to taste

water

Marinate mushrooms in Nama Shoyu and olive oil while preparing the rest of the ingredients. Add all other ingredients to food processor, then add marinated mushrooms. Process until well blended and smooth, adding only as much water as necessary. You will need to keep scraping down the sides. Form into elongated ½ inch tall patties and dehydrate at 145 degrees for 2 hours, then at 110 degrees for 4 to 5 hours or until they will hold together. When done they will have a slight crust on the outside and be moist on the inside. Serve warm from dehydrator or re-warm them in dehydrator before serving. Serves 4.

Serving suggestion: make a thick raw vegetable soup and use as a sauce.

PART 11
SNACKS AND FINGER FOODS

Here are some ideas for what to eat when you are hungry and only want something quick and small, or are wondering what to serve at a party.

Banana Chips

What to do with lots of ripe bananas. These are like eating candy, so don't be afraid to make a lot!

Advance prep: None

Ripe bananas

Slice bananas into ¼ inch thick rounds or lengthwise strips. Place on dehydrator screens and dehydrate at 110 degrees until chewy. Great travel food. Makes about 15–20 round chips per banana.

HORS D'OEUVRE IDEAS

- Peel and slice **Kohlrabi** into finger-food sized pieces. Top with a dollop of **Pâté** (see pâté section, page 107) and half an **olive**.

- Slice **zucchini, mushrooms, or Jicama** and top with **Pâté** of your choice.

- Slice **radishes** and top with **Pâté** of your choice.

- Top **Corn Chips** (see page 81) with a bit of **Guacamole** (see page 125).

- Top small dehydrated **Crackers** with **tomato** and **sprouts.**

- **Swiss Chard Rolls** made in small sizes (see page 127).

- Sliced **Nori Rolls** (see page 130).

- Cut in half and hollow out a large red or yellow **bell pepper**, fill with **Pâté**. Cut **veggie strips** to dip in Pâté.

- Fill **mushroom caps** with **Almond Ricotta** (see page 103). Dehydrate on screens for 1 hour at 145 degrees (or eat as is).

- Fill a bowl with **Veggie Chips** (see page 138).

- Set out a bowl of fresh **sugar snap peas**. Sometimes the simplest things are the best.

Tomato/Walnut Crème Dip

Advance prep: 6 hours to soak walnuts, 10 minutes to soak dried tomatoes

1 avocado
½ cup walnuts, soaked
½ cup dried tomatoes, soaked 10 minutes
½ clove garlic (or to taste)
dash of Italian Blend seasoning
2 teaspoons Nama Shoyu
2 teaspoons lemon juice
Krystal Salt to taste
water to blend

Blend all in Vitamix to be a coarse, thick consistency, being careful to not add too much water. It is best if the tomatoes are not completely blended. Makes about 2½ cups.

Use as a dip for veggies or raw crackers or thin to use as a salad dressing.

Veggie Chips

These can be used as wonderful snack foods or as an addition to a regular meal. Experiment to see which flavors you like best.

Advance prep: None

Suggested vegetables to use:
Eggplant
Zucchini or any summer squash
Tomatoes
Winter squash
Yams or sweet potatoes

Slice veggies thinly with the exception of tomatoes—they need to be sliced about ½ inch thick. Yams, sweet potatoes and some kinds of winter squash, sliced with a Mandoline that makes very thin slices, are very tasty dehydrated until dry or just by themselves. Top veggies with one of the following toppings if desired and dehydrate at 145 degrees for 1 hour (dry tomatoes at 145 degrees for 2 hours) then at 110 degrees until crispy or chewy, as desired.

TOPPINGS IDEAS

Here are some ideas for different flavored toppings:

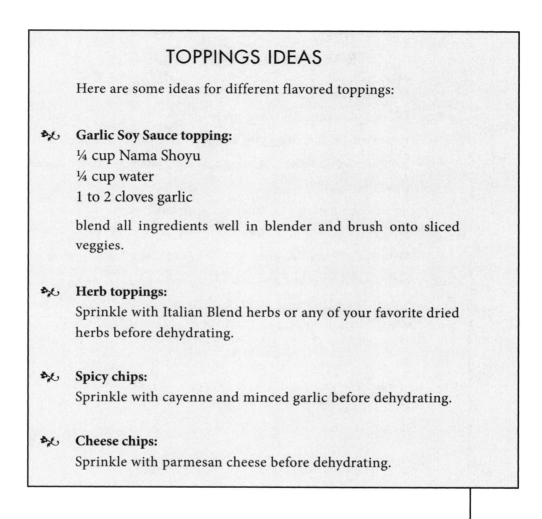

❧ **Garlic Soy Sauce topping:**
¼ cup Nama Shoyu
¼ cup water
1 to 2 cloves garlic

blend all ingredients well in blender and brush onto sliced veggies.

❧ **Herb toppings:**
Sprinkle with Italian Blend herbs or any of your favorite dried herbs before dehydrating.

❧ **Spicy chips:**
Sprinkle with cayenne and minced garlic before dehydrating.

❧ **Cheese chips:**
Sprinkle with parmesan cheese before dehydrating.

TRAVEL/TRAIL FOOD IDEAS

- Dehydrated crackers
- Buckwheat Crunchies (see page 38)
- Hard veggies such as carrots, kohlrabi, jicama, cut in slices
- Nuts and seeds, soaked or bring a jar for soaking overnight while traveling.
- Soaked almonds, peeled and eaten with Goji berries are a powerful super-food combo.
- Dehydrated tomatoes or Veggie Chips (see page 138)
- Dehydrated bananas (see page 135)

PART 12
DESSERTS

Desserts have always been a specialty of mine. I have included lots of dessert recipes here to show that you don't have to give up your favorite comforting sweets when eating live food. But lest you think I thought up all these yummy foods just for others, I must confess that my main motivation was to have them for myself! Subsequently, fudge, ice creams, and more, were created to the delight of me and my friends. Hopefully they will delight you, too.

Pecan Fudge

This recipe tastes absolutely decadent! Your friends will be impressed, even those who think they don't like raw foods.

Advance prep: 2 or 3 hours to soak dates (depends on the softness of the dates you use)

1 cup pecans, not soaked or soaked then dried
½ cup walnuts, not soaked or soaked then dried
½ cup pine nuts (This recipe can be any combination of
    these 3 nuts)
½ cup carob powder
¼ cup raw cocoa powder (can also be all carob powder)
¾ cup dates, pitted and soaked until soft in just enough
    young coconut milk or water to barely cover
1 tablespoon vanilla extract
1 teaspoon almond flavor
½ teaspoon Krystal Salt brine
sesame seeds

Grind pecans and walnuts as fine as possible. In large bowl, stir nut powder, cocoa and carob powder together, smashing any lumps. In a separate small bowl, blend pine nuts, dates, vanilla and almond flavor with hand blender. Mash wet into dry ingredients, using hands if necessary. Form into small balls and roll in sesame seeds. If the mixture is not stiff enough to form into balls, refrigerate several hours first. The firmness will vary with how much oil is in the nuts and how much water is used to soak the dates. Makes about 3½ cups.

For Christmas fudge, soak dates in fresh orange juice and add a half teaspoon orange zest to the wet ingredients.

To soak dates: Pit, press into a jar or bowl and add only enough water to barely cover so there is no excess liquid that needs to be drained off after soaking. Too much water will make the fudge too soft.

Pistachio Fudge

Using all carob powder allows the flavor of the pistachios to come through.

Advance prep: 2 or 3 hours to soak dates (depends on the softness of the dates you use)

2 cups pistachios, finely ground
⅓ cup carob powder
¾ cups dates, pitted and soaked in young coconut water or
      water until soft
1 teaspoon vanilla extract
½ teaspoon Krystal Salt brine

In a large bowl, stir ground pistachios and carob powder together, smashing any lumps. In separate small bowl blend dates, vanilla and salt, with hand blender. Mash date mixture into nuts and carob powder to make a stiff dough, using hands, if necessary. Form into small balls or eat as is by the spoonful. If the mixture is not stiff enough, refrigerate it for a few hours. Makes about 3 cups.

To soak dates: Pit, press, press into a jar or bowl and add only enough water to barely cover, so there is no excess liquid that needs to be drained off after soaking.

Mesquite Fudge

An interesting variation of fudge.

Advance prep: 2 or 3 hours to soak dates (depends on the softness of the dates you use)

1 cup walnuts, not soaked, or soaked and dried

½ cup pine nuts, not soaked, or soaked and dried

½ cup almonds, not soaked, or soaked and dried

½ cup dates, pitted and soaked until soft with only enough
　　　　water to barely cover

¼ cup raw mesquite meal

¼ cup raw carob powder

1 tablespoon vanilla extract

1 teaspoon almond extract

½ teaspoon Krystal Salt brine

Grind nuts as fine as possible. In a large bowl, stir nuts, mesquite meal, and carob powder together until well blended, mashing any lumps. In a small separate bowl, blend dates, vanilla, almond extract and salt with hand blender. Add wet ingredients to dry using hands to mix, if necessary. Form into balls and roll in chopped macadamia nuts (or covering of your choice), if desired. Makes about 3½ cups.

To soak dates: Pit and press into a jar or bowl and add only enough water to barely cover, so there is no excess liquid that needs to be drained off after soaking.

Marzipan Balls

It is good that this is such a simple recipe as these will be eaten very quickly!

Advance prep: none

1 cup almonds, unsoaked or soaked and dried, ground fine
about ½ cup honey
raw cocoa powder, about ¼ cup

Place ground almonds in mixing bowl and add only enough honey to form a stiff mixture. You may need to use your hands. Form into small balls (about ¾ inch diameter) and roll in cocoa powder. Keeps several days in refrigerator. Makes about 18 balls.

For a real Marzipan flavor, soak the almonds at least 6 hours, peel them, and then dehydrate until dry again. If you don't want to go to all that work, this recipe still tastes very good with unpeeled almonds.

Almond Banana Confection

Simple and sweet! A bit like Marzipan but without as much honey.

Advance prep: none

2 cups almonds, not soaked or soaked and dried, ground
     fine
1 large banana
3 Tablespoons honey

Blend banana and honey with hand blender then add to ground almonds and mix well. Refrigerate for several hours to make mixture firm enough to form into small balls. Roll in ground almonds if desired. Makes about 25 balls.

Fig Delights

These are nice in the fall, around holiday time

Advance prep: none

1 cup chopped dried figs
1 cup pine nuts
¼ cup Sucanat
½ teaspoon orange zest
1 teaspoon vanilla extract
½ teaspoon cinnamon, plus some for dusting

Combine everything but the Sucanat in food processor. Remove from processor and fold in Sucanat by hand. Form into small balls and dust with extra cinnamon. Makes about 22 balls.

Sesame Fudge Cookies

Fudgey and satisfying on many levels! Good energy food for hiking.

Advance prep: 6 hours to soak seeds, 2 hours to soak dates, dehydrating time

1 cup sesame seeds, soaked
½ cup carob powder (or part raw cocoa powder)
meat from 1 young coconut (optional)
1 large or 2 small ripe bananas
1 cup dates, pitted and soaked in only enough water to
    cover
2 droppers-full liquid Stevia (optional)
½ teaspoon Krystal Salt brine
coconut milk from young coconut (optional)
water to blend

Blend all ingredients well with enough coconut milk and/or water to turn over. It will take a strong blender (Vitamix), or perhaps blending only half at a time. Drop by spoonfuls onto Teflex dehydrator sheets and dehydrate at 145 degrees for one hour then at 110 degrees until chewy. They will be quite thin. Remove from Teflex sheets when dry enough to hold together and place on screens to complete drying. Makes about 27 cookies.

Oreos

These do take a bit of work to prepare ahead of time, but are totally worth it and very fun to grab from the freezer and eat.

Advance prep: Sesame Fudge cookies, freezing time

Sesame Fudge cookies (see page 147)

Crème center:
¾ cup young coconut meat
¼ cup pine nuts
2 tablespoons honey
½ teaspoon vanilla extract
water for blending

Blend together in a Vitamix coconut meat, pine nuts, honey, vanilla and only enough water to make a thick crème. Spread a thin layer onto a Sesame Fudge cookie then top with another cookie, old fashioned "Oreo" style. Place them on a covered plate in the freezer until frozen. Enjoy them frozen from the freezer. Makes about 14 cookies.

Persimmon Cookies

These are truly a fall delight!

Advance prep: 6 hours to soak nuts, 2 hours to soak dates, dehydrating time

4 ripe persimmons, cut into 1 inch cubes
1 ripe banana, cut into pieces
3 cups pecans, soaked
½ cup dates, pitted and soaked in only enough water to
        cover
2 teaspoons vanilla
½ teaspoon Krystal Salt brine

Blend all ingredients, including date soak water, in food processor until smooth. Drop by spoons-full onto Teflex sheets and dehydrate for 2 hours at 145 degrees, then at 110 degrees until chewy. Turn them over and place on screens when they are dry enough to hold together, to speed drying time. Makes about 25 cookies.

As a variation, add 1 teaspoon cinnamon.

Pineapple Coconut Cookies

Yum! is all I can think of to say about these. You really should try them.

Advance prep: dehydrating time

2½ cups chopped pineapple
1 cup raw cashews
¾ cup dates, pitted and packed
meat of 1 young coconut
½ teaspoon Krystal Salt brine

Process all in food processor until smooth. Drop by spoonfuls onto Teflex dehydrator sheets and shake to flatten a bit. Dehydrate for 2 hours at 145 degrees, then at 110 degrees until chewy. Turn them over and place on screens when possible, to speed drying time. Makes about 25 cookies.

Mesquite Cookies

Advance prep: 6 hours for soaking seeds, dehydrating time

1 cup sesame seeds, soaked
 3 small or 2 medium bananas
½ cup mesquite powder
½ cup soft dates, pits removed
2 droppers-full liquid Stevia (optional)
½ teaspoon Krystal Salt brine

Process all ingredients several minutes in food processor. Drop by spoonfuls onto Teflex sheets of food dehydrator and flatten slightly. Dehydrate for 2 hours at 145 degrees then at 110 degrees until chewy. Turn them over and place on screens when they are dry enough, to speed drying. Makes about 20 cookies.

Angel Pudding

A good dessert or snack in the fall and winter when apples are fresh and crisp.

Advance prep: none

4 large apples
meat of 1 young coconut
6 dates, pitted (or to taste)
1 tablespoon vanilla
milk of young coconut to blend

Remove apple cores, cut in pieces and put into blender along with the other ingredients. Blend all to smooth consistency. Serves 2–3.

Banana Macadamia Cream

This makes a very rich tasting pudding. Be sure macadamia nuts are fresh as they don't keep long once they are shelled.

Advance prep: none

4 bananas
1 cup macadamia nuts, not soaked
⅓ cup dates
1 teaspoon vanilla
water or young coconut milk

Put all ingredients in blender with just enough water to blend. Serves 4.

Carob/raw cocoa powder can be added as a variation for a rich chocolate fudge pudding taste.

Chocolate Pudding

I love this recipe because it is so simple and the ingredients are always readily available. Even if all you have on hand are bananas and carob powder, it still tastes great. It is a wonderful evening snack when you are hungry but don't want to eat anything too heavy.

Advance prep: none

4 ripe bananas
meat of 1 young coconut (optional)
6–8 dates, pitted
2 tablespoons carob powder (or raw cocoa powder)
½ teaspoon vanilla
¼ teaspoon almond extract
water or coconut milk

Blend all, adding enough water or coconut milk for the desired consistency. Serves 2.

Carob/Chocolate Sauce

Great as a topping for raw ice cream and pies. Maple syrup is not raw, but this is so much better than store-bought chocolate sauces, it feels worth including.

Advance prep: none

1½ cups maple syrup
½ cup carob powder (or raw cocoa powder, or combination)
1 tablespoon vanilla extract
½ teaspoon almond flavor
1 tablespoon olive oil

Blend everything well in blender. Keeps well in the refrigerator for a long time. Makes about 2 cups.

As a variation, add dates to thicken and dip strawberries in, wow! Sure to be a hit at parties.

Orange Zimt Sauce

Zimt is cinnamon in German. Pour this sauce over pies, cakes or just sliced fresh fruit for an easy dessert.

Advance prep: 6 hours to soak nuts, 2 hours to soak dates

½ cup almonds, soaked
¼ cup dates, pitted and soaked with only enough water to
    cover
juice of one orange
pinch orange zest
¼ teaspoon cinnamon
water

Combine everything in a blender, including date soak water, adding enough water for desired consistency. Blend until very smooth. Makes about 1½ cups.

Mesquite Coconut Crème Cake

Mesquite meal gives a rich earthy flavor to this cake usually made with carob powder.

Advance prep: 6 hours to soak nuts

1 cup pecans, soaked
1 cup pine nuts, not soaked
⅓ cup raw mesquite pod meal (carob powder also works)
½ cup pitted soft dates (if they are not soft, soak in a little
    water)
2 droppers full liquid Stevia (optional)
½ teaspoon Krystal Salt brine
sliced strawberries, peaches or bananas

Grind nuts, dates, Stevia and brine in food processor until smooth. Place in bowl and mix in mesquite meal, using hands if necessary. With wet hands flatten onto an oiled plate and form into desired shape. (A heart is nice!) Top with sliced fruit then spoon on the Coconut Crème (see page 158) and smooth as you would frosting. Refrigerate or freeze until firm. Serves 6.

Coconut Crème

Advance prep: None

¾ cup young coconut meat
¼ cup pine nuts
2 tablespoons honey
1 dropper full liquid Stevia (optional)
Enough coconut milk or water to make a thick crème in
    blender or Vitamix

Blend to a smooth consistency and spread on cake. Serves 6 when
spread on Mesquite Coconut Crème Cake (see page 157).

No Fail Pie Crust

This crust is so good it almost doesn't matter what you put on top of it. It's a no-fail recipe!

Advance prep: 6 hours to soak nuts

1 cup almonds, soaked
1 cup pecans or walnuts, soaked
2 cups dates, soaked if they are not soft ones
1 tablespoon vanilla

Grind nuts first in food processor, then add dates. You may need to scrape down the sides occasionally. Press into pie plate with wet hands. Top with sliced seasonal fruit of your choice. Serves 8 with filling.

Serve with a side bowl of Carob/Chocolate Sauce (see page 155) to dribble on top of the fruit.

PART 13
ICE CREAM

Live food ice cream! It is worth the investment in an ice cream maker to be able to make these luscious desserts. These have all the yumminess of the dairy version without the unhealthy fat, sugar and pasteurized milk, or the processed aspects of the soy/rice varieties. The addition of a raw egg yolk makes them creamier and adds a good quality raw protein, lecithin, and vitamin B12, but is not necessary for these desserts to satisfy all your ice cream cravings. You are in for a delightful surprise . . .

Pistachio Ice Cream
Perhaps the closest to real dairy ice cream you will taste! It will amaze all your friends, too.

Advance prep: none

½ cup pistachios
2 cups water
2 medium to large bananas
½ cup dates, pitted
1 raw egg yolk (optional)
½ teaspoon Krystal Salt brine
2 droppers-full liquid Stevia (optional)

Blend pistachios with 1 cup water for 1 minute. Add remaining ingredients and blend until smooth. Freeze according to ice cream maker instructions. Makes 3½–4 cups.

Cashew Pineapple Ice Cream

*This recipe can be made without the coconut but is creamier with it.
It will not freeze as firm with the coconut, however.*

Advance prep: none

heaping ½ cup raw cashews
1 cup water
½ cup coconut milk or water
2 heaping cups chopped, peeled pineapple
½ cup packed pitted dates
1 banana
½ teaspoon Krystal Salt brine
meat of 1 young coconut (optional)
1 raw egg yolk (optional)

Blend cashews and 1 cup water for 1 minute. Add remaining
ingredients and blend until smooth. Freeze according to your
ice cream makers instructions. Makes 3½–4 cups.

Strawberry Banana Ice Cream

Advance prep: 6 hours to soak nuts

½ cup almonds, soaked
1½ cups water
2 ripe bananas
1 heaping cup strawberries, washed and green tops removed
½ cup dates, pitted
1 raw egg yolk (optional)
½ teaspoon vanilla extract
½ teaspoon Krystal Salt brine
2 droppers-full liquid Stevia (optional)

Blend almonds with 1 cup water for one minute. Add remaining ingredients and blend until smooth. Freeze according to ice cream maker instructions. Makes 3½–4 cups.

Blueberry Ice Cream

A nice colorful blue ice cream.

Advance prep: 6 hours to soak nuts

½ cup almonds, soaked
1¾ cups water
1 large banana
1 cup fresh blueberries
½ cup packed pitted dates
1 raw egg yolk (optional)
½ teaspoon Krystal Salt brine
2 droppers full of liquid Stevia (optional)

Blend almonds and 1 cup water for 1 minute. Add remaining ingredients and blend until smooth. Freeze according to ice cream maker's instructions. Makes 3½–4 cups.

Carob Banana Ice Cream

Advance prep: 6 hours to soak seeds

heaping ½ cup sunflower seeds, soaked
1¾ cups water
2 small bananas
½ cup packed pitted dates
¼ cup carob powder
1 raw egg yolk (optional)
1 teaspoon vanilla extract
½ teaspoon almond flavor
½ teaspoon Krystal Salt brine
2 droppers full of liquid Stevia (optional)

Blend sunflower seeds with 1 cup water for 1 minute. Add the remaining ingredients and blend well. Freeze according to ice cream maker instructions. Makes 3½–4 cups.

Mango Ice Cream

Advance prep: 6 hours to soak nuts

½ cup almonds, soaked
1¾ cups water
½ cup packed pitted dates
2 large mangoes, peeled and cut off pit
1 raw egg yolk (optional)
½ teaspoon Krystal Salt brine
2 droppers-full liquid Stevia (optional)

Blend almonds with 1 cup of water for at least 1 minute. Add remaining ingredients and blend until smooth. Following machine instructions pour into ice cream maker and freeze. Makes 3½–4 cups.

Cashew Vanilla Ice Cream

Advance prep: none

½ cup cashews, slightly heaping
2 cups water
2 bananas
½ cup dates
½ teaspoon Krystal Salt brine
½ teaspoon vanilla extract
2 droppers-full liquid Stevia (optional)

Blend cashews and 1 cup water for 1 minute. Add remaining ingredients and blend well. Freeze according to electric ice cream maker's instructions. Makes 3½–4 cups.

SOURCES

Krystal Salt: Available through various websites and most natural food stores

Websites for **hard to find organic raw foods** and superfoods:

www.rawfood.com

www.eatraw.com

www.rawganique.com

www.rawtimes.com

www.treeoflife.nu

www.livesuperfoods.com

www.living-foods.com

Harmonizers to protect against EMF's: For information, write to Mary Rydman at rydman@gmx.net. Read about them on www.originalradiance.com.

Amazon Herbs: Health-supportive herb formulas and high quality skin care using products from the Amazon Rainforest: For more information, write to Mary Rydman at rydman@gmx.net

Raw organic dates, grains, nuts, carob powder and seeds for sprouting:
Jaffe Bros.

760-749-1133

www.organicfruitsandnuts.com

Non irradiated raw **hemp seeds**: Available through Manitoba Harvest company, widely available in natural food stores.

Blue Green Algae: www.klamathvalley.com. Information also available from Mary Rydman at rydman@gmx.net.

Emotional Body Enlightenment (EBE): www.theohumanity.org

Recommended Reading

Barron, Daniel. *There's no Such Thing as a Negative Emotion*. Outskirts Press, 2006.

Barron, Daniel. *Enheartenment: Embodiment of the Divine Human*. Outskirts Press, 2006.

Boutenko, Victoria. *Green for Life*. Raw Family Publishing, 2005.

Cousens, Gabriel. *Rainbow Green Live-Food Cuisine*. Berkeley, CA: North Atlantic Books, 2003.

ABOUT THE AUTHOR

Mary Rydman left her former career as a commuter airline pilot for Skywest Airlines in 1993 to study health and nutrition, and is the co-founder of Original Radiance, which offers a new paradigm for physical health and nutritional healing. She holds two black belts in Korean martial arts and teaches Radiant Life Qigong. Since 2001, Mary has been practicing EBE (Emotional Body Enlightenment)—a spiritual work that helps us inhabit our humanity through the healing of the emotional body and uncover emotional sources of un-health.

For more information about Mary's work, please visit *www.original radiance.com*. She can also be reached through e-mail at *rydman@gmx.net*.

MY OWN RECIPES

MY OWN RECIPES

_____

_____

_____

_____

_____

_____

_____

_____

_____

_____

_____

_____

_____

_____

_____

_____

_____

_____

_____

_____

_____

_____

_____

MY OWN RECIPES

MY OWN RECIPES

MY OWN RECIPES

MY OWN RECIPES

_____

_____

_____

MY OWN RECIPES

MY OWN RECIPES

MY OWN RECIPES

MY OWN RECIPES

MY OWN RECIPES

MY OWN RECIPES

MY OWN RECIPES

MY OWN RECIPES

_____

_____

_____

_____

_____

_____

_____

_____

_____

_____

_____

_____

_____

_____

_____

_____

_____

_____

_____

_____

_____

_____

MY OWN RECIPES

_____
_____
_____
_____
_____
_____
_____
_____
_____
_____
_____
_____
_____
_____
_____
_____
_____
_____
_____
_____
_____
_____